a summertime GRILLING GUIDE

from The Splendid Table

by LYNNE ROSSETTO KASPER and SALLY SWIFT

authors of How to Eat Supper *and* How to Eat Weekends

AMERICAN PUBLIC MEDIA™ | American Public Media
St. Paul, Minn.

A Summertime Grilling Guide From
The Splendid Table®

Copyright © 2012 Minnesota Public Radio.

Published in the United States by American Public Media,
producer of the radio program /
The Splendid Table

St. Paul, Minn.

www.splendidtable.org

www.minnesotapublicradio.org

www.americanpublicmedia.org

Art Direction and Design by Tracy Kompelien

Creative Direction by J. Zachary Keenan

Project Management by David Edin

Produced by Marybeth Anderson

Copyedited by Luke Taylor

Index prepared by Elizabeth Parson

Photographs by Terry Brennan / Brennan Photography Inc.

Food Styling by Lara Miklasevics / Hero Food Styling, LLC

Library of Congress Cataloging-in-Publication Data

Kasper, Lynne Rossetto

A Summertime Grilling Guide from The Splendid Table – 1st ed.

p. cm.

Includes index.

ISBN 978-0-9855370-0-5 (pbk.)

1.   Cooking.   2. Barbecue cookery
I. Swift, Sally II. Splendid Table (Radio program)   III. Title.   IV. Title: A Summertime Grilling Guide

Also by LYNNE ROSSETTO KASPER & SALLY SWIFT

The Splendid Table's How To Eat Supper (Clarkson Potter, 2008)

The Splendid Table's How To Eat Weekends (Clarkson Potter, 2011)

Also by LYNNE ROSSETTO KASPER

The Splendid Table® (William Morrow, 1992)

The Italian Country Table (Scribner, 1999)

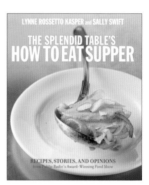

dedication

For David Edin, a man who knows how to light a fire
and have fun doing it.

ACKNOWLEDGEMENTS

Like all things sustainable, this project would never have come together
without the will of many people. Thank you to Jennifer Luebke and
Jennifer Russell, the core of our Splendid Table family, and welcome
to our newest members: Jennifer Larson, Mary Beth Leone Getten,
Chris Peters and Andy Kruse. Thank you for slipping into our tight-knit
group so gracefully. To Judy Graham, a woman who always manages to
seem elated when shipped a manuscript, no matter what the deadline.
Thank you for your keen eyes and devotion over these many years and
may we have many, many more together.

To the team that pulled this project together in a record three months' time:
Marybeth Anderson, David Edin, Zachary Keenan, Tracy Kompelien,
Bridget Murphy, Luke Taylor and John Pearson, photographer Terry
Brennan, stylist Lara Miklasevics, Teresa Thell and Elizabeth Parson.
What a pleasure to work with such professionals; can we please do more?

We are lucky to be a part of an amazing creative community at American
Public Media; thank you to Peter Clowney, Judy McAlpine, and Danielle
Stellner for constant glass-half -full support and to our esteemed colleagues,
we may be ships passing in the night, but boy is it great when we meet up.

table *of* contents

Introduction

Grilling season is officially open. Even if you live where grilling season never ends, there is something about early summer that sends even the most fire-phobic into the great outdoors with tongs in hand. In our 2012 edition of *A Summertime Grilling Guide*, we're out to spark your imagination as well as give you some basic tools that will guarantee success every time you step up to the grill. Summertime eating should be about retiring anything complicated or demanding and bringing out all the simplicity you can muster. Think about the utter ease of passing a beautiful bowl of fresh radishes with good sea salt, slicing up a perfect peach for dessert, tossing bright tasting salads full of fresh herbs, wrapping a lettuce leaf around a piece of grilled meat before dipping it in garlicky hummus, and eating with all-out pleasure. It's unstuffiness at its best.

If ever there was a time of year to try eating local and tracking down organic ingredients, summer is it. With farmers' markets going great guns, we can buy organic produce and other foods directly from the person who grew or created them. It's a win-win situation from so many points of view — freshness, taste, health, education, price and support for your local economy.

Flip these pages for fast weeknight dishes as well as party food, and along the way, discover some new tastes and concepts. Nearly every country grills, and this summer we want to give you a quick culinary tour. The variety should keep everyone happy, from vegans to carnivores.

If grilling hasn't entered your life yet, or you want to brush up your skills, many of the essentials are covered. You'll find guides to picking the grill that's right for you, how to judge fuels, how to make a fire and the tricks to cooking over it with confidence. We hope this griller's guide to good eating brings you a season of great times with family and friends.

Lynne and Sally

Essential Equipment: Which Grill is Right for You?

Gas or charcoal? The debate has gone on for ages and will doubtless continue. Most pros wouldn't think of using anything but a charcoal grill, but each type has its merits and steadfast supporters.

The one thing that both sides of the aisle do agree on is size, and the larger the better. A large grilling surface allows you to move the food around from hotter parts to cooler parts — so you can do fast browning over high heat, then move on to a cooler area to finish the cooking without burning the outside of the food. And that cooler temperature helps cook things evenly; no more raw centers with overcooked exteriors.

Then there's the grill-to-griller body match. This doesn't have to be a blind date. We rarely stop and consider what that grill is going to feel like when we work with it. Before buying, handle the grill, the lid, the rack and the controls. Think about what you have to do to start the fire and to clean up afterwards. Think about height and weight. Will you need to be constantly bending over? Will you need a crane to move it? If you match your grill to your body structure and comfort zones, you'll have a lot more fun using it.

Here's a list of pros and cons for each type of grill to help you decide which suits your lifestyle and how you cook.

Charcoal Grills

PROS:

Cost less than gas grills.

Can use both wood and charcoal, which is the only way to get authentic smoky, grilled flavor.

It's easy to add even smokier flavor by adding wood chips to the fire — like hickory, apple, oak and mesquite — which you've soaked in water or juiced.

Makes a hotter fire and allows for several heat intensities, depending on how many coals you use and how they are distributed in the grill. And a hotter fire gives a crusty brown exterior when you want it.

CONS:

Heat control is more challenging. Some fires burn hotter than others, and the longer the fire burns, the weaker it becomes unless you keep adding charcoal, a process that can be clumsy depending on the design of the grill. Some have liftable sections that let you easily slip in coals, but adding fuel can also produce some intense smoke until the new charcoal ignites.

Requires steady attention tending the coals and extinguishing flare-ups.

Slower and messier to light and heat up. You have to wait for the coals to be ready for cooking.

Clean-up takes time, and you need a fireproof container for spent coals and ash.

Gas Grills

PROS:

Convenient and easy to use. Simply push a button to start the grill and turn a knob to adjust the heat.

Cleaner to operate than charcoal grills.

Less fuel is used with less fussing around to keep the fire going. You can grill for hours on one tank of fuel.

Easier to read and adjust temperatures as some models have an exterior thermometer.

Indirect grilling is easier on a gas grill, provided you have at least two burners. With three or four burners you can easily duplicate the multiple heat zones that are possible with a charcoal grill.

CONS:

Until you get into more expensive high-end models, some gas grills don't get hot enough for quick high-heat searing.

Unless the grill has a smoker box (usually on pricier models), it can be difficult to get the smoky flavor that is the heart of grilling. But there's an easy fix for this: soak your wood chips in water, wrap them in heavy-duty foil, punch a few holes for the smoke to escape and put the packet directly over a burner set at high heat and let the smoke begin.

grilling essentials

The Art of the Fire

What Type of Fuel to Use: Our top pick is hardwood, such as oak, cherry, hickory, apple or mesquite. Actual wood gives wonderful flavor, even when you are not smoking (and when soaked in water, wood will produce fragrant smoke). Wood chunks are sold in bags much like charcoal. Find them in natural food stores, hardware stores, garden centers, supermarkets and kitchen shops. With luck, you may know someone with a fallen tree and you can chop your own.

A close second choice is hardwood charcoal, also labeled "lump charcoal" or "charwood."

Charcoal briquettes are a very distant third choice. They're often composed of compressed coal dust, borax and petroleum binders, none of which we need in our food or the environment.

Starting the Fire: Chimney starters now have it all over the old lighter-fluid technique. Aside from its sometimes explosive nature, lighter fluid smells and tastes nasty, and does nothing for the environment.

The chimney is a metal cylinder with a handle and it's ridiculously easy to use. There's a grate in the middle of the cylinder where you stuff a couple of sheets of crumpled newspaper and top it with the wood or charcoal. Remove the rack from the grill and set the chimney where the charcoal goes. Light the paper and the charcoal catches fire. Once the coals are red, turn them onto the bottom grate of the grill.

Creating Cooking Zones: The way you spread out the coals can open up cooking possibilities.

For fast direct cooking of small pieces of food, spread out the red-hot coals in a single layer, or pile them in one zone that takes up about a third of the space. The empty area is your safety zone where you do slow cooking or stop overcooking.

If you want to sear and then slowly cook things like burgers, steaks and vegetables, you will need two cooking zones. Pile coals 4 inches deep on one side of the grill for high heat, and layer in a single layer on the other side for low heat. Now you have the same flexibility as you have on a stovetop, except that instead of changing the temperature under the food, you move the food to the level of heat you want.

When you are slow-roasting something like ribs, whole chickens and roasts, you want the coals pushed away from the center of the grill, leaving a bare spot so you have indirect heat. Place a drip pan in that center opening. This gives you a large cooking surface with varying heat levels.

How Hot are the Coals?

Recipes often tell you to wait for a grey ash to form over the coals, but this doesn't apply to all dishes. A good way to determine the temperature is to hold your hand 5 to 6 inches above the cooking grate. You'll know how high the heat is by how long you can hold your hand over the grate.

1 to 2 seconds: high heat

3 to 4 seconds: medium heat

5 to 6 seconds: low heat

General Grilling Guidelines

For juicier meats, poultry and fish, brining is the way to go. Heavily season a brine and you'll have juiciness plus flavor permeating the meat. This is an especially good way to bring tenderness to tougher, inexpensive cuts. If you'd like, you could brine, then marinate or use a dry rub — or do all three for more complex flavors.

Marinades flavor and tenderize only the surface of meats. Dry rubs do the same thing. Both open up flavor possibilities. Just don't overdo it when you have great-tasting food to begin with. Let nature shine through.

To reduce flare-ups, trim excess fat from chops and steaks to no more than 1/4 inch. Grilling with the lid on also reduces flare-ups while cooking food faster and more evenly.

Move meat around on the grill with a spatula, not a barbecue fork. Poking meat will cause the juices to escape. And resist the urge to press down with your spatula, especially when cooking hamburgers (see Burger Tips, page 25). They won't cook any faster and you'll squeeze out the flavorful juices.

Use grilling times only as a guide. There are variables like the thickness of the food you are cooking, whether the food is cold or at room temperature when it goes on the grill, and even the weather. Allow more time at high altitudes or on windy or cold days. Keep an instant-read thermometer handy to check for doneness.

Brush sauces and glazes that contain sweeteners on the food during the last 15 or so minutes of grilling to avoid burning.

Use clean tongs and spatulas to remove cooked food from the grill, and never place cooked food on the same platter you used to carry raw food to the grill.

When cooking cuts of meat, make sure the surface is dry before putting the meat on the hot grill. You want it to sear, not steam.

Most vegetables can be cooked on a grill, with the general rule of thumb being to grill them quickly and over direct medium to medium-high heat.

Marinate or toss vegetables with seasonings and oil before cooking to boost flavor and prevent sticking to the grill grate.

Cut larger vegetables like eggplant, zucchini and summer squash, carrots, and sweet and white potatoes into uniform lengthwise slices about 1/4- to 1/2-inch thick to increase the surface area exposed to the grill. Cut onions and bell peppers into wedges and place directly on the grate or thread onto skewers. Wooden skewers can be found in most supermarkets in the housewares aisle. Don't be tempted to skip soaking them in water; they will catch on fire! If you have metal skewers, they'll work, too.

Thoroughly oil the grill grate before grilling.

Be sure to place the grill several feet away from the side of your house, deck floor and railing. (Take this from a woman [Lynne] who almost burned out the canvas awnings of a neighbor's house.) Never grill in the garage or on a covered patio or porch with a deep overhang. Make sure the grill is stable and sits on a flat surface. Keep an eye on little ones, roll up your sleeves, and save that chic but billowing little number for another time.

Is It Done Yet?

Use an instant-reading thermometer and the chart below to determine when meats and poultry are done to your liking. Remember, everything needs about 10 minutes to rest once it's off the grill to settle juices and finish cooking. Temperatures go up about 5°F, so remove meats when a little underdone.

120°F: Rare. For those convinced this is the only way to eat steak. Raw was the stop before this.

125° to 130°F: Medium-Rare. For our taste, the perfect doneness for steak and lamb.

135° to 140°F: Medium-Rare to Medium. Still moist with lots of flavor.

145° to 150°F: Medium-Well. Heading to dry. With beef and lamb, this is only for those who insist.

150° to 160°F: Well Done. 150°F is ideal for pork.

165°F: Ideal for stewed meat.

170° to 180°F: Only for poultry.

L to R: Ranch Dressing, Somalian Bizbaz Sauce, West Indies Spice Blend

marinades, rubs, SAUCES & dressings

A Marinade Guide

Please remember these are suggestions and ideas, not etched-in-stone recipes. Making homemade marinades is a good way to begin trusting your *own taste*, so sample as you put them together and vary measurements and ingredients as you like. They're a snap to pull together, have none of the dubious ingredients in commercial versions, and can be inexpensive to do at home once you have gathered the ingredients.

Marinades and sauces containing sweeteners like sugar, honey, or molasses will burn quicker than those without sweeteners. Watch them closely, and move whatever you're grilling to indirect heat if it starts to burn.

Depending upon the recipe and if time allows, meats could be marinated in the refrigerator for anything from 45 minutes to overnight. Don't marinate soft vegetables longer than 10 minutes as they will throw off water and become soggy before they ever touch the grill. Hard vegetables like potatoes, carrots, etc., can marinate for up to 30 minutes.

The Balsamic Cheat

There is a neat trick you can do to inexpensive balsamic vinegar. You can make it taste more like the densely rich and delicious pricey balsamic by boiling it down to a syrup in a skillet or saucepan with a little brown sugar. Figure 1 to 3 tablespoons sugar per cup of inexpensive balsamic, depending on how acidic it might be. The syrup keeps in the fridge for months.

BASIC ASIAN MARINADE: Purée together a 2- to 3-inch piece fresh ginger, 4 large garlic cloves, and 1/3 cup *each* soy sauce *and* rice wine or dry sherry. Optional ingredient is 2 to 5 tablespoons sugar; another is Chinese Five Spice powder or 1 star anise, broken.

BASIC MEDITERRANEAN MARINADE: Blend together 2 minced large cloves of garlic with 1/3 cup fresh lemon juice, 1/3 cup good-tasting extra-virgin olive oil, a tablespoon of fresh rosemary or oregano leaves, and salt and pepper to taste.

BASIC MEXICAN MARINADE: Stem and seed 4 to 6 large dried mild to medium hot red chiles (Ancho, Guajillo or New Mexican). Soak them for 30 minutes in hot water to cover.

Drain the chiles and purée them in a blender with 2 large garlic cloves, 1/3 cup orange juice, 1/4 cup canola oil, 1 teaspoon dry oregano (preferably Mexican) and enough water to make a thick, creamy consistency. Season to taste with salt and pepper. Perfectionists strain the marinade before using it.

BASIC SOUTHEAST ASIAN MARINADE: Purée together the pulp and juice of 1 medium lime, a 2-inch piece of fresh ginger, 3 to 4 large garlic cloves, 2 teaspoons to 1 tablespoon Asian fish sauce, 8 branches fresh coriander or 1/2 cup fresh mint leaves, 2 to 3 tablespoons sugar and 1/2 teaspoon freshly ground black pepper. Add very hot fresh Thai chiles, or milder Serrano or jalapeños to taste.

ITALIAN BALSAMIC MARINADE: Blend together 4 minced large garlic cloves, 1/3 cup *each* balsamic vinegar *and* good-tasting extra-virgin olive oil, 1/4 to 1/2 teaspoon freshly ground black pepper, and 1 tablespoon dry or 10 leaves fresh basil. (See Sidebar: The Balsamic Cheat.)

SIMPLIFIED HOT JERK MARINADE: Purée together 1 fresh scotch bonnet or habanero chile (use gloves to handle these searingly hot beauties) with 1/4 cup *each* of good-tasting extra-virgin olive oil *and* cider or wine vinegar, half an onion and 1 generous teaspoon *each* of thyme, allspice, black pepper *and* cinnamon.

Concocting
Spice Blends & Rubs

A dry rub is the fast solution to flavoring virtually everything you cook —
from seafood, to steak, to chicken, to veggies and tofu. Even ten minutes
of letting a rub settle into a piece of fish before it's grilled can take it into
a new realm. And the spice rub doubles as a seasoning blend for anything
else you're cooking. Add it to salad dressings, soups, dips, sautés — you
get the idea.

Sure, you can buy pre-made spice rubs, but your own blends will taste
brighter (they're fresher), cost less and give you exactly what you like
because you're doing them to your taste.

> **TIP:** *If you have any doubt about which spices go together, put a little of
> each on your tongue. You'll know immediately if the combo works or not.*

Head to the spice aisle or bulk spice area of your supermarket, pick
out several combinations of seasonings you like and blend up a couple
of batches.

Whole spices that you grind yourself deliver the biggest flavors for your
money. (And the spices you haven't ground yet will keep their character
for a year, versus pre-ground spices which hold for about 3 months).
Grind them in a clean coffee grinder or mortar and pestle.

If you've only got pre-ground spices, it's not a tragedy; your blends will
still work. Just sniff spices before using for the robust aromas that mean
they are still fresh enough to deliver lots of flavor.

Whether using whole or pre-ground spices, store your blends in airtight
containers, and keep them in the refrigerator or freezer.

On the facing page are some combinations we've found especially
successful. If using pre-ground spices, use the same measurements used
here for whole spices.

Lynne's Global Spice Blend

Think of this as a foundation to build into other cuisines. For instance, evoke Morocco by adding a little sweet paprika and cinnamon; head to India with the addition of more coriander and black pepper; and channel your inner Mexican by adding more chile and cumin.

Grind together 2 tablespoons whole cumin seed with 1/4 cup whole coriander and 1 tablespoon black peppercorns.

WEST INDIES SPICE BLEND: Grind together 2 generous teaspoons whole allspice, 1-1/2 teaspoons whole coriander seed, 1 teaspoon black peppercorns, and a 2-inch piece of cinnamon stick, broken. Stir in 2 tablespoons sweet paprika, 1 generous tablespoon dry basil, 1/2 teaspoon dry thyme, and 1-1/2 teaspoons ground ginger.

TINGLY SPICE BLEND: For those times when a little spice is called for. Blend 1 tablespoon hot chili powder (or to taste), 2 tablespoons brown sugar, 3 tablespoons ground cumin, and 4 tablespoons ground coriander.

TANDOORI SPICE BLEND: India's famous yogurt-spice marinade for chicken roasted in special clay ovens can season anything on the grill or in the pot. This is the spice blend part of the equation. Keep it on the shelf and use it at will. Add the yogurt whenever you'd like. Red food coloring is traditional in tandoori, but not essential.

Grind together 1 teaspoon each whole cloves, black peppercorns and ground turmeric with 1-1/2 teaspoons each cardamom seeds (removed from their husks), cumin seed, broken cinnamon stick, fennel seed, ground ginger and ground pure chile (mild to hot depending upon your taste).

Sauces and Dressings

You cannot escape the aisles and aisles jammed with bottled sauces and dressings. We consider it a luxury to be able to just shake and pour, right? Well, luxury has its price. If you take the time to scroll through the lists of ingredients on those bottles, we bet you will put them right back on the shelf — and rightly so. Not only are they packed with preservatives and fillers, they are expensive and usually disappointing. With a couple of minutes spent in the kitchen, you can concoct delicious versions all on your own. Best of all, you can customize a dressing with what's already in the fridge — it's the perfect opportunity to put those little bits and dabs of leftover condiments in the fridge door to work.

On the following pages are some of our summer standbys.

Sweet-Tart BBQ Sauce

Once you have tasted a homemade version of classic American BBQ sauce, you will never go back. Most BBQ sauces are essentially a simmered tomato sauce, redolent with spices and vinegar and given the sticky lip-smacking addition of something sweet. A small amount of prep brings this sauce together in a snap. Riff off it however you please. Maybe you'll end up bottling your own.

Canola oil

2 medium onions, minced

1/4 teaspoon salt

3 large garlic cloves, minced

1 teaspoon freshly ground black pepper

2 teaspoons ground allspice

2 3-inch cinnamon sticks, broken

1 teaspoon ground cloves

1/2 teaspoon ground ginger

2 tablespoons sweet paprika

1 cup pineapple juice

1 cup cider vinegar

2 28-ounce cans whole tomatoes, puréed

2 tablespoons tomato paste

1-1/3 cups (packed) dark brown sugar

1 tablespoon Tabasco sauce

1 tablespoon Worcestershire sauce

1/4 cup grainy dark mustard

1/2 cup molasses

1 stick unsalted butter

MAKES

8

CUPS

COOK TIME

20 minutes prep time; 50 to 60 minutes stove time

Keeps refrigerated up to 2 weeks, and freezes for 6 months.

1. Coat the bottom of a 6-quart pot with a thin film of oil. Set it over medium-high heat and sauté the onions with the salt until they are golden brown. Stir in the garlic, pepper, allspice, cinnamon, cloves, ginger, paprika, pineapple juice, and cider vinegar. Cook down to just a thick glaze on the bottom of the pan.

2. Add the tomatoes, tomato paste, sugar, Tabasco, Worcestershire, mustard, molasses, and butter. Cook at a slow bubble, uncovered, for 50 minutes or until thick. Taste for seasoning, remove the cinnamon stick and store or use.

Somalian Bizbaz Sauce

This cool, pale-green sauce of lime, chile and coriander was inspired by Somali chef Jamal Hashi. Every day he makes a bowl of it for his Safari Express food stand in Minneapolis' Global Market, and every day, he runs out. Jamal remembers this sauce in Somalia, where people made it with what grew in their backyards — the ubiquitous lime trees, chile and coriander.

We eat it with everything — burgers, corn on the cob, fried plantains, meats, salad, fish, and any vegetable.

MAKES

1¹/₂

CUPS;
DOUBLES
EASILY

COOK TIME

20 minutes
prep time;
1 hour
refrigerated
rest time

Store
covered in
refrigerator
for 1 to
3 days.

1 large **garlic clove, crushed**

Juice of half a large **lime**

1/2 to 2 **whole fresh Serrano chiles (depending on your taste)**

1/2 to 2/3 **tight-packed cup fresh coriander leaves**

1 to 2 teaspoons **sugar, or to taste**

1/2 cup **low-fat plain Greek yogurt**

Salt and freshly ground black pepper to taste

More lime juice if needed

1. Place the garlic clove in a coffee cup and squeeze the lime juice over it. Let stand 20 minutes while you gather the other ingredients.

2. Place the garlic, lime juice, chile, coriander leaves, sugar, yogurt, salt and pepper into the bowl of a food processor and purée. Taste for balance. Refrigerate the Bizbaz an hour or so to mellow, and use cool.

Classic Vinaigrette Dressing

This is the true Italian or French dressing — so basic, it's scary. But when made with a good-tasting vinegar and a flavorful oil, this dressing is a star.

This is the base you use to make Dijon dressing, Bleu Cheese, Ranch, anything your appetite desires.

Find a pint jar (2 cups) with a screw top. You're making this by taste, not by exact measurement, so the quantities are approximations; and be sure to taste as you go. This is about what tastes good to you.

1/2 cup **good-tasting vinegar (i.e. a blend of rice vinegar and balsamic, or cider, wine or sherry vinegar)**

1/2 cup **good-tasting extra-virgin olive oil**

Salt and freshly ground black pepper to taste

1. Combine the vinegar and oil in the jar, shake, taste, and then add more oil or vinegar to balance. Season with salt and pepper to taste.

variations:

Herbs & Garlic: Add freshly chopped or dried herbs and minced garlic to the basic dressing, or rub the salad bowl with a crushed clove of garlic then add the herbs directly to the bowl with the greens.

Dijon Dressing: Pour about 1/2 cup of the dressing into the bottom of a large salad bowl, add a generous tablespoon of Dijon mustard, some fresh tarragon and 1 shallot, minced. Blend with a fork, add the greens and toss.

Honey Mustard Dressing: Add to Dijon Dressing brown sugar or honey to taste. A tablespoon of mayonnaise makes it creamy.

French Bleu Cheese Dressing: Take a little classic vinaigrette, blend in bleu cheese and garlic to taste.

Creamy Bleu Cheese: Add sour cream, mayonnaise and minced onion to French Bleu Cheese Dressing.

Ranch Dressing: Add classic vinaigrette, minced garlic, chopped parsley, chopped scallions, and chopped basil with equal amounts of mayonnaise and buttermilk and mix well.

MAKES

2

CUPS;
DOUBLES
EASILY

COOK TIME

5 minutes
prep time

Store covered in the refrigerator up to a week. Use at room temperature, shaking to blend before using.

main
DISHES

Cumin-Lemon Lamb Grill in Lettuce Rolls with Grilled Vegetables

Essential Grilled Steak with Chopped Fresh Summer Herbs

SERVES

2 *to* 4

MULTIPLIES
EASILY

COOK TIME

10 minutes
prep time;
10 minutes
grill time

The crusty char of grilled beef dressed with a mince of bright fresh herbs and a little good-tasting olive oil is a natural for summer. Even if those herbs aren't growing on your windowsill or in the yard, they're selling for next to nothing at a farmers' market. This is a simplified version of Italy's gremolata (there, it's made with a mince of lemon peel, herbs, and garlic). Since summer eating is all about simplicity, use whatever combination of herbs you have around, and add a squeeze of fresh lemon to heighten flavors even more.

You can do this recipe with any steak: rib eye, Porterhouse, T-bone, New York strip, Delmonico, or the delicious money saver, a tender cut of chuck steak. But do look for a thick cut, at least 1-1/4 inches and ideally 1-1/2 to 1-3/4 inches, which can be carved into slices and anointed with the herbs and oil.

Serve with New Potato Salad (page 62) and Grilled Asparagus and Spring Onions (page 69).

1 pound steak such as rib eye, Porterhouse, T-bone, New York strip, Delmonico, or the tender part of a chuck steak, cut at least 1-1/4 inches thick, trimmed of excess fat

Salt and freshly ground pepper to taste

1/2 cup lightly packed minced fresh herbs, such as parsley, dill, tarragon, thyme, rosemary, marjoram, cilantro, lovage, and sorrel, in any combination

Good-tasting extra-virgin olive oil

Salt and freshly ground pepper to taste

1 large lemon, cut into 6 wedges (optional)

1. Prepare a charcoal grill for two-zone cooking (page 4). If using a gas grill, set one burner on high and one burner on low. Oil the grate.

2. Season the steaks generously with salt and pepper on both sides and set aside.

3. Combine the minced herbs with salt and pepper to taste and set aside.

4. When the grill is ready, place the steak over the hottest part of the fire for 6 to 7 minutes, taking care not to move the steak around too much to ensure a nice char. Turn the steaks over using tongs and grill the second side over lower heat, turning occasionally, for about the same amount of time, to desired doneness (see cooking chart, page 7). The best way to make sure the steak is done to your liking is to insert an instant-reading thermometer into the thickest part of the meat, not touching bone. Let the steak rest, loosely tented with foil, about 10 minutes.

5. When ready to serve, carve the steak across the grain into 1/2-inch slices and transfer to a platter along with any juices. Sprinkle the slices generously with the fresh herbs, drizzle on a little olive oil and serve.

Grilling, broiling, barbecuing – whatever you want to call it – is an art, not just a matter of building a pyre and throwing on a piece of meat as a sacrifice to the gods of the stomach.

— *James Beard*, Beard on Food *(1974)*

**Essential Grilled Steak with
Chopped Fresh Summer Herbs**

Cider-Grilled Pork Steaks

Put aside the pricey pork chop every now and then and turn to a cheaper cut with a lot more character: the pork steak. In today's world of über-lean pork, the pork steak, which is cut from the generously marbled shoulder, is so notoriously succulent it's a natural for the grill. Here the steaks are bathed in a marinade of apple cider and maple syrup, which turns sticky and crispy on the grill.

Serve these steaks up with something fresh like Summer Greens & Melon Salad (page 57) or Dandelion and Caramelized Carrot Salad (page 50).

SERVES

4 to 6

COOK TIME

10 minutes prep time; 30 minutes to 4 hours in marinade; 15 minutes grill time

2 pounds **pork steaks (from shoulder or butt), cut 1-inch thick and trimmed of excess fat**

5 tablespoons **maple syrup**

3 tablespoons **cider vinegar**

5 large **cloves garlic**

1/2 teaspoon **freshly ground black pepper**

Salt to taste

1. Spread the pork steaks on a large platter. In a blender or food processor, purée together the maple syrup, cider vinegar, garlic, and pepper. Pour over the steaks, turning them to coat with the mixture. Marinate the steaks in the refrigerator for 30 minutes to 4 hours.

2. Prepare a charcoal grill for two-zone cooking (page 5). If using a gas grill, set one burner on high and one burner on low. Oil the grate.

3. When the coals are ready, sear the steaks on both sides over high heat, sprinkling them with salt. Move them to the cooler side of the grill and continue cooking them slowly until they are firm when pressed with your finger, about 5 to 8 minutes more per side. Rest the steaks off the fire for 10 minutes and serve them hot.

The Secret to Cooking Protein

In this season of "toss it-on-the-grill, get a char, and finish cooking fast," there's a basic rule of thumb that's good to remember: The slower you cook proteins, the more juiciness, tenderness and flavor you get. So sear over high heat to get a beautiful charred surface, but finish cooking low and slow to ensure tenderness, whether it's a steak, a piece of fish, or a soy cutlet.

Burger Tips

Flavorful meat is the first step to a great hamburger. Choose ground chuck or sirloin (never ground round) that's at least 85% lean to 15% fat.

Handle ground beef gently. Over-mixing when blending other ingredients into the meat gives you tough burgers and less flavor. A few pats are all that's needed to form patties.

Keep the juices in the meat by not pressing down on the patties or piercing them during cooking.

Cover the grill while the burgers are cooking so the meat retains the smoky flavor from the charcoal. It wouldn't hurt to throw some soaked fruitwood chips on the fire, either. For safety, cook burgers to an internal temperature of at least 160°F. Use an instant-reading thermometer to check.

Brush the buns with a little melted butter and grill for about a minute, or until the inside surface is toasted and golden.

The New Summer Burger

Here's our new summer burger, packed with a ton of flavor and so juicy you could skip the ketchup.

Not to knock the great American burger, but they get boring after a while. Meatloaf patties are never boring because you can keep switching out ingredients as you please. Besides, give a meatloaf mix the right kind of backup, like this one with a little bacon, cheese, and breadcrumbs soaked in wine and garlic, and you get a patty so moist it's nearly impossible to dry out on the grill.

> **COOK TO COOK:** *Fool around with these seasonings. Add a teaspoon of Tingly Spice Blend or Global Spice (page 13). Work in leftover grilled vegetables that you've minced up. Nearly anything goes. Just keep the bacon, cheese and bread for moisture.*

MAKES
4 to 7
patties:
HALVES or DOUBLES EASILY

COOK TIME
20 minutes prep time; 12 to 15 minutes grill time

1 large **garlic clove**

1/2 cup **cubed (about 1/4-inch cubes) whole-wheat baguette, or other whole-grain chewy bread**

1/4 cup **dry red or white wine**

3/4 teaspoon **salt**

1/4 to 1/2 teaspoon **freshly ground black pepper**

1 tablespoon **balsamic vinegar**

1 tablespoon **tomato paste**

4 large **fresh basil leaves, torn**

1 slice **bacon, minced**

1/2 cup (1-1/2 to 2 ounces) **shredded Asiago or extra-sharp Cheddar cheese**

1/4 medium **onion, cut into 1/4-inch dice**

1/4 large **sweet red pepper, cut into 1/4-inch dice**

2 large **whole scallions, thinly sliced**

1 large **egg yolk**

1 pound **ground 85% beef chuck**

Buns and trimmings as you'd like

1. Prepare your grill for a two-zone fire. If using a gas grill, set one burner on high and one burner on low.

2. Turn on a food processor and drop in the garlic. Then drop in the bread cubes and process until pieces are a quarter the size of a pea. Scrape everything into a large bowl and moisten the crumbs with the wine. Let wine soak into the bread while you prep the rest of the ingredients.

3. Completely blend in all the remaining ingredients except the meat. Then work in the meat with a spoon or fork until everything is thoroughly mixed. Scoop up 2- to 3-inch balls and shape them into 3- to 5-inch patties (I like my burgers no more than 3/4-inch thick since they will be cooked to medium-well). Dent them in the middle for even cooking.

4. Oil the grill and set the burgers over the hot fire. Sear them on both sides, turning gently with a spatula. Shift them over to lower heat and cook about 5 minutes more per side, or until an instant-reading thermometer inserted in their centers reads 160°F. Remove the patties to a clean platter to rest for 5 minutes. Serve them hot on cut-up baguettes or buns.

Cumin-Lemon Lamb Grill in Lettuce Rolls with Grilled Vegetables

SERVES

4

COOK TIME

30 minutes
prep time;
30 minutes
to 12 hours
marinating
time;
20 minutes
grill time

A lovely thing about this dish is that it can be a meal for vegetarians or carnivores alike, and nothing says summer like eating with our fingers. Eating outside means we have permission to pick up all sorts of things — from chicken wings and hot dogs to these lamb–and vegetable–filled roll-ups. This is the way it works: Set out a pile of lettuce leaves, a pile of fresh herbs, some ground chile, a bowl of store-bought chickpea dip (hummus), and some instant chive-yogurt sauce. Heap the grilled vegetables on one platter, the cooked lamb on another.

To eat, spread a lettuce leaf with chive-yogurt sauce, add a few pieces of lamb, top them with fresh mint and maybe some chile. Roll up and taste the mix of hot, cool, fresh, and tangy all in each bite. Possible combinations go on.

This dish is wonderful paired with Golden Rice Salad (page 54).

> **COOK TO COOK:** *Chicken thighs and pork shoulder can be substituted for the lamb. And don't marinate the vegetables as some will throw off water and become soggy before they ever touch the grill.*

SPICE PASTE/MARINADE:

3 to 4 large **garlic cloves**

Pulp of 1 large **lemon (cut away all zest and white pith), seeded**

2 teaspoons **sweet paprika**

2 teaspoons **ground cumin**

1/2 teaspoon *each* **coarse salt** *and* **freshly ground black pepper**

MEAT:

2 1/2 to 3 pounds **lamb steaks cut from the leg (or other tender cut), trimmed of fat and cut into strips about 1/2-inch thick by 2 to 3 inches long**

VEGETABLES:

4 medium **zucchini, cut into 3/4-inch by 3-inch unpeeled strips**

2 medium **red onions, sliced into 3/4-inch by 3-inch strips**

2 large **yellow peppers, cut into 3/4-inch by 3-inch strips**

INSTANT CHIVE-YOGURT SAUCE:

2 cups whole-milk yogurt

1/2 cup thinly sliced chives, or whole scallions

GARNISHES:

Juice of 1/2 lemon

1 large or 2 small heads Bibb lettuce, whole leaves washed and dried

10 to 12 sprigs fresh mint

10 to 12 sprigs fresh coriander

1/4 to 1/3 cup Aleppo chile, or other medium-hot pure chile powder

2 cups homemade or store-bought Middle Eastern chickpea dip (hummus)

1. In the bowl of a small food processor, purée together all the spice paste ingredients. Place the lamb in a medium bowl and toss with half of the paste. Place the vegetables in a large bowl and toss them with the remaining paste.

2. Make the Instant Chive-Yogurt Sauce by blending the yogurt and chives together. Set out the sauce with all the garnishes except the juice from the half lemon.

3. Prepare a charcoal grill for one-zone direct grilling (page 5), or preheat a gas grill to high.

4. When the fire is very hot, begin by grilling the vegetables first. Spread them on the grill and cook about 2 to 5 minutes per side, or until they are browning but still have a little crispness to them. Take care not to burn them. With tongs, lift them to a serving platter.

5. Grill the lamb strips 1 to 2 minutes on one side, turn with tongs, then grill 1 to 2 minutes on the other side. You want the interior to be very pink. Cut into a piece to check. Remove the meat to a serving platter. Squeeze the juice of half a lemon over the meat. Set the vegetables and lamb out and invite everyone to create their own lettuce rolls.

Cast-Iron Pans on Outdoor Grills

A grill is a great place to put your cast-iron pans to work. Instead of producing fire-alarm smoke inside, just move your heavy-duty searing to the great outdoors. Make the fire as hot as you can and place the pan directly on the grate as the fire is building up heat.

Cast-iron cookware stands tall in the quality-for-money category. When buying cast-iron, there are some features to look for: The pan should be thick and heavy, and the surfaces and edges should be very smooth. Two quality manufacturers are Griswold and Lodge (which comes pre-seasoned). Both companies make a wide variety of pieces. Pick them up online or in many hardware stores.

Seasoning Cast Iron: When you get a new pan home, scrub it with a steel wool pad to get rid of the sticky surface coating designed to protect the pan prior to purchase. Set the pan over very low heat until it's thoroughly dry, coat it generously with a flavorless vegetable oil, then place the pan in the oven preheated to 300°F and leave it for several hours.

Turn off the heat and leave the pan in the oven over night. Lightly rinse the pan with hot water, wipe out the moisture, dry over very low heat, rub it with oil, and again place it in the oven to "bake" for several hours.

After the pan is seasoned, clean it after every use with hot water only (try not to use soap), wipe it out, and dry over very low heat.

As you use the pan, it will become more and more non-stick, but if anything does stick to the surface, scrub it off with salt. Because cast-iron is brittle, each time you use the pan, start with moderate heat to warm the pan gradually, then increase the heat if you need to.

Weeknight Kofta with Allspice and Almonds

The haunting scent of allspice balanced with bright lemon juice and flecks of nuts make these Middle Eastern kofta (meat patties) hard to resist. This recipe is Sally's savior as she lives with a major carnivore (exactly the opposite of how she likes to eat). She uses 80% to 85% ground chuck, but because there is so much flavor here, you can use leaner meat and still have no fear of cooking them to well done as recommended. Serve them with simple brown jasmine rice or the Golden Rice Salad (page 54), and a spoonful of Cucumber Yogurt Salad (page 60).

COOK TO COOK: *It's hard to judge the spicing of raw ground meat as you should never taste it raw. Instead, make a trial patty, cook it up, taste (the perk of being the cook), and adjust the seasoning as needed.*

SERVES
2 *to* **3**
DOUBLES EASILY

1 pound **80% to 85% ground chuck, or other ground meat as desired**

3 tablespoons **tomato paste**

1/2 cup **minced onion**

Grated zest of half a large lemon

Juice of half a large **lemon**

2 teaspoons **allspice**

1/2 teaspoon **cayenne, or more to taste**

1/4 cup **chopped blanched almonds or pine nuts**

Salt and freshly ground black pepper to taste

Good-tasting extra-virgin olive oil

ACCOMPANIMENT:
CUCUMBER YOGURT SALAD (PAGE 60)

COOK TIME

15 minutes prep time; 20 minutes grill time

Can be made ahead and stored covered in the refrigerator until ready to grill. Makes delicious leftovers.

1. Make the kofta: Place all the ingredients except the salad in a large bowl and knead with your hands until well combined. Firmly form the mixture with your hands into 2-inch, slightly flattened patties and set aside. (They need to be firmly formed or they will break apart when you cook them.) You can make the kofta ahead at this point and store loosely covered in the refrigerator overnight.

2. Prepare a charcoal grill for two-zone cooking (page 5). If using a gas grill, set one burner on high and one burner on low.

3. When the coals are at medium heat, generously oil the grill. Place the kofta on the grill, taking care not to crowd them, cooking them in batches if necessary. Let them cook thoroughly on one side before flipping them and cooking the other. It is important not to move them around too much so they don't break apart. Pull them from the grill when there is no pink interior and their centers have reached 160°F on an instant-reading thermometer.

Tabasco Sweet-and-Tart Glazed Wings

SERVES
4 *to* **6**

COOK TIME
10 minutes
prep time;
2 days
refrigerated
marinating;
1-1/2 to
2 hours
grill time

Keep up
to 5 days
covered
in the
refrigerator;
reheat
nicely;
excellent
hot,
at room
temperature,
or cold.

Sweet, tart and snappy with healthy shots of hot sauce, and grilled to near potato chip crispness, in our book the chicken wing approaches celestial perfection. Neither light meat nor dark, they are a coupling of both, and nothing pulls in flavor and crisps up in cooking quite like wings. It's that wonderful proportion of luscious skin to meat and bone.

Give these wings plenty of marinating time and keep your fire low so most of their fat cooks off as the skin crisps. One last thing: no "drummies," please. This recipe is for the entire wing because each of its three sections is a different eating experience. Serve up these wings with Cucumber Stick Salad (page 58).

COOK TO COOK: *Grilling guru Steven Raichlen, author of* The Barbecue Bible! *(Workman, 1998) and other titles on grilling, suggests this ingenious tip to ensure the maximum amount of crispy skin: Before marinating the wings, arrange them on long bamboo skewers, starting at the wing tip and threading the skewer through the wing so it lies flat and straight.*

3 tablespoons **soy sauce**

1/2 cup **cider vinegar**

1/4 cup **dry white wine**

1/4 cup **good-tasting extra-virgin olive oil**

1/4 cup **Tabasco sauce, or more to taste**

6 large **cloves garlic, minced**

1 cup **apricot jam**

3 to 4 pounds **chicken wings with wing tips, rinsed**

Fresh mint (optional)

1. Two days before cooking, combine all ingredients except the wings in a bowl. Taste for hot/sweet/sour/salt balance, and adjust to your preference. Flavors should be strong.

2. Pierce each wing in several places with a knife to help the marinade penetrate. Place the wings in heavy plastic zip-top bags and divide the marinade between them. Seal and refrigerate 2 days, turning bags occasionally for even marinating.

3. Two hours or so before serving, set up the charcoal grill for three-zone indirect grilling so you have a hot zone and a medium-hot zone, with most of the cooking area in the low heat zone. Do this by piling the preheated wood charcoal deepest against one side of the grill so the pile diminishes toward the center. If using a gas grill, heat to high to sear the wings, then lower the heat to medium-low.

4. When the coals are ready, drain the wings from their marinade, saving the marinade in a saucepan. Oil the grate and spread the wings out on the grill. You want to move them around so they lightly sear over the hot area, then move them to the low heat area. If using a gas grill, sear all the wings over high heat then lower it to medium-low.

5. Cover the grill and keep the fire at medium-low by adjusting the vents. Cook the wings, turning often and checking for burning, about 90 minutes, or until they are crisp and their meat is tender.

6. As the wings cook, boil the marinade for 5 minutes, adding 1/2 cup water to it. In the last 30 minutes of grilling, baste the wings with the marinade. You want them glazed but not burnt. Serve the wings piled on a platter lined with a bed of fresh mint, if possible (nothing beats the combination of chiles and sweet mint). Serve with extra Tabasco on the table for those who believe it's never hot enough.

A perfect summer
day is when the
sun is shining,
the breeze is blowing,
the birds are singing,
and the lawn mower
is broken.

— *James Dent*

Essential BBQ Chicken

This is a summer essential: sticky, crispy barbecued chicken that comes together in less than 20 minutes. An ideal lazy-man's recipe, here's a technique that puts to rest once and for all the ornery side of grilling cut-up chicken: one piece is raw at the center while another piece is turning to cinders. Instead, oven-roast the chicken ahead, so when it hits the grill all it needs is warming and anointing with a good BBQ sauce. While any will do, we recommend you give our Sweet-Tart BBQ Sauce (page 15) a try. It is well worth the additional effort. Serve this chicken with Tijuana Cole Slaw (page 63) and a pile of napkins .

COOK TO COOK: *You can marinate and roast the chicken a day ahead and store it loosely covered in the refrigerator. Bring it to room temperature before grilling.*

1/2 cup **dry white wine**

1/4 cup **apple cider vinegar**

6 large **garlic cloves, minced**

1 tablespoon **packed dark brown sugar**

Salt and freshly ground pepper

3-1/2-pound **chicken, cut into 8 pieces**

2-1/2 cups **Sweet-Tart BBQ Sauce (page 15)**

1. Combine the wine, vinegar, garlic, sugar, salt and pepper in a zip-top plastic bag large enough to hold all the chicken. Add the chicken to the marinade, turning the pieces to coat them. Refrigerate for 4 to 6 hours.

2. Preheat the oven to 350°F. Drain the marinade into a small bowl. Pat the chicken dry and spread out the pieces in a shallow roasting pan. Roast for 45 minutes to an hour, or until the center of the breast reads 165°F on an instant-reading thermometer. As the chicken cooks, baste it during the first half of the cooking time with a cup of the marinade, then baste with pan juices. Remove the chicken from the oven and either set it aside while you ready the grill, or refrigerate it for up to 24 hours. Have the chicken close to room temperature when you're ready to grill.

3. Prepare a charcoal grill for one-zone cooking (page 5), or preheat a gas grill to medium. Allow the charcoal fire to burn down to a white ash, moderate heat or lower (page 5), and oil the grate.

4. Place the chicken pieces on the grill and baste liberally with the BBQ sauce. Cover and cook, turning and basting occasionally with the sauce. The chicken should be sticky and crisp, with an internal temperature of 170°F. Depending on how cold the chicken is when it hits the grill, this can take 15 to 20 minutes. When fully heated through, pile the chicken on a platter and serve. Pass the remaining BBQ sauce for extra gilding.

main
dishes

SERVES

4

DOUBLES
EASILY

COOK TIME

15 minutes
prep time;
30 to 40
minutes
oven time;
15 minutes
grill time

Ginger Hoisin Summer Shrimp

This is summer finger food — a big pile of shrimp that you peel and eat with your fingers only needs lots of napkins. Shrimp stay juicier when grilled in their shells, and the short marinating time heightens their character. Serve them hot, warm, or lightly chilled with Cucumber Stick Salad (page 58).

For the marinade, you want the dark, fragrant, Asian sesame oil that is used as a flavoring, not the lighter one that is used for sautéing and for things like salad dressings.

MARINADE:

1/2 inch piece of fresh ginger, peeled and minced

2 large garlic cloves, minced

1/2 teaspoon freshly ground black pepper

3 tablespoons soy sauce

3 tablespoons hoisin sauce (available in the Asian section of many supermarkets and in specialty food stores. Koon Chun brand is especially reliable)

1 teaspoon dark Asian sesame oil

1 teaspoon sugar

2 tablespoons Chinese rice wine, dry sherry, or dry white wine

SHRIMP:

2 pounds extra-large shrimp (11 to 15 per pound), not shelled, but with legs removed, rinsed and patted dry

Oil for the grill

2 whole scallions, thinly sliced (optional garnish)

1. Combine all the marinade ingredients in a large bowl. Add the shrimp and gently toss to coat with the seasonings. Refrigerate 30 to 40 minutes.

2. Prepare a charcoal grill for two-zone cooking (page 5). If using a gas grill, set one burner on high and one burner on low.

3. Brush the grate with oil and place the shrimp on their sides, about an inch apart, over the hottest part of the fire. Quickly brush them with any remaining marinade then count to 30. Turn them right away with tongs and move them away from the highest heat.

4. Finish cooking the shrimp until they turn pink and are barely firm, about 3 minutes. Do not overcook. Immediately remove to a platter and scatter with the scallions.

SERVES

4 *to* **6**

COOK TIME

15 minutes prep time; 30 to 40 minutes marinating time; 6 to 10 minutes grill time

About Shrimp

Shrimp from North American waters are generally preferred from both a sustainability and quality standpoint. As a general rule, follow the recommendations of the Monterey Bay Aquarium's Seafood Watch program (www.seafoodwatch.org). The program rates wild-caught prawns and spot shrimp from British Columbia a "best" choice. Wild-caught prawns and spot shrimp from the United States are rated "good," as are white, pink and brown shrimp (farmed or wild) from the United States. Check before buying as these ratings can change.

Check out www.wildamericanshrimp.com for a list of Certified Wild American Shrimp. As of this writing, the site lists these brands of frozen shrimp to look for in grocery stores: Arista, Caught Fresh, Dominick's Frozen Shrimp, Emeril's Louisiana Shrimp, Sea Pearl, and SeaPak Shrimp Company.

Smoke Roasting

Anything you roast in the oven is even better cooked outside with a little smoke. Think whole fish, chicken, pork roasts, lamb and, of course, the Thanksgiving bird. There are a couple of tricks to know, which we learned from long-time griller John Willoughby.

Make sure you have a lidded grill that is at least 22 inches in diameter. According to John, smoke roasting is all about indirect heat. John says people use "way too many coals," when all you need is about 3 or 4 handfuls, or enough to fit in a shoe box.

To maintain steady heat, replenish the coals every 30 minutes.

Recipes like the Smoky Salmon Steaks (facing page) or Essential BBQ Chicken (page 35) are good places to try wood chips, scavenged grape vines or fruitwood trimmings.

Smoky Salmon Steaks

It's no surprise that the richness of salmon takes beautifully to the flavor of wood smoke. But what is a surprise is that you don't need hours of smoking to bring out those great tastes. In this recipe, we speed up the smoking process by rubbing the fish with Spanish smoked paprika, and then slowly roasting the fish over wood chips. The salmon comes off the grill beautifully burnished and tinged with the scent of wood smoke. Try the fish with our bright green Somalian Bizbaz Sauce (page 16).

COOK TO COOK: *Salmon steaks are easiest to handle on the grill, but steaks or filets of any full-flavored fish can stand in here as well.*

1 cup **wood chips, soaked for at least an hour in water to cover**

1 tablespoon **smoked Spanish paprika**

2 teaspoons **sea salt**

1 teaspoon **sugar**

4 **salmon steaks** (about 3 pounds)**, or the equivalent weight in filets**

Somalian Bizbaz Sauce (page 16) (optional)

1. Prepare your grill for a two-zone fire. If using a gas grill, set one burner on high and one burner on low.

2. Combine the smoked paprika, sea salt, and sugar in a small bowl and mix well. Rub both sides of the steaks with the seasoning mix and set aside.

3. When the coals are medium-hot, oil the grate generously on the side with the lower heat, taking care as the fire will flare up. Toss half the wood chips on the hottest part of the fire and quickly place the salmon steaks on the oiled, lower-heat side. Cover with the lid, making sure that the vents are at least half open.

4. Grill 3 to 4 minutes. Open the grill and toss the remaining wood chips on the fire, (slipping them through the larger hole by the grill handles if your grill does not have a liftable, hinged grate). Carefully turn the steaks with a spatula, returning them to the coolest side of the grill, cover, and continue cooking another 3 to 4 minutes until the steaks are firm to the touch when pressed in the center. The salmon should still be red, not pink, in the center. Make a small slit with the tip of a knife to check. Do not overcook. Pull from the fire and let rest 5 to 10 minutes.

main dishes

SERVES
4

PREP TIME
5 minutes
prep time;
one hour
soaking time
if using
wood chips;
10 to 15
minutes
grill time

Hot Spiced Portobello Grill with Fresh Arugula and Parmigiano Shavings

This is a lovely, light vegetarian supper. The preparation is simple because, quite frankly, the meatiness of the mushrooms against the cool, delicate greens and the mellowness of good cheese cannot be bested.

SERVES
4 to 5

COOK TIME
15 minutes
prep time;
10-12 minutes
grill time

1/2 cup **good-tasting extra-virgin olive oil**

2 large **garlic cloves, or more to taste**

1/2 teaspoon **hot red pepper flakes, or more to taste**

1/2 to 1 **teaspoon dry oregano**

8 to 10 **large Portobello mushroom caps**

Salt and freshly ground black pepper to taste

1 tightly packed cup **fresh baby arugula leaves**

3 ounces **Parmigiano-Reggiano cheese, shaved with a vegetable peeler**

Juice **of** 1/2 to 1 whole **lemon**

1. In a blender, purée together the olive oil, garlic, pepper flakes, and oregano. Brush both sides of the mushrooms with the oil blend. Set the rest of the oil aside to finish the dish.

2. Prepare a charcoal grill for one-zone direct grilling (page 5) or preheat a gas grill to medium.

3. Allow the charcoal fire to burn down to white ash, moderate heat and cook the mushroom caps on both sides until tender all the way through and slightly crisp, turning often and taking care not to burn them, 5 to 6 minutes per side or until the mushrooms are nicely browned with some crisp edges. Season with salt and pepper to taste.

4. Immediately set the caps on a serving platter. Top with the arugula, then the cheese shavings, sprinkle with the reserved oil and finish with fresh lemon juice. Serve right away to get the impact of hot mushrooms and cool, fresh greens.

Ginger-Grilled Miso Eggplant on Crispy Kale

I used to think grilling eggplant was about karma, and I didn't have any. Charred on the outside, raw on the inside was my destiny. Everything changed with two discoveries by Sally: this lusciously spiced ginger-miso sauce *and* microwaving eggplant slices before they hit the grill. You cannot mess this up, no way, no how. (Why it never occurred to me, I'll never know.)

Bed down those slices on the crisp grilled kale (another revelation) and you have a sensational vegan main dish.

> **COOK TO COOK:** *There are hundreds of versions of miso (fermented soybean pastes from Japan). They each have their own distinctive taste, though they are generally broken down into light or dark varieties. Generally, the lighter the miso the sweeter it tastes. Misos are inexpensive, they keep a long time in the refrigerator, and they bring a lot of bang for the buck. So pick some up, and put them to work in soups and dressings.*

SERVES

4

DOUBLES EASILY

COOK TIME

10 minutes prep time; 2 to 4 hours for marinating at room temperature; 10 minutes grill time

This dish is good hot off the grill or at room temperature.

1/2 cup **light (yellow or white) miso**

1/4 cup **mirin (sweetened Japanese rice wine)**

2 tablespoons **rice wine vinegar**

3 tablespoons **minced ginger**

2 teaspoons **sugar**

2 tablespoons **vegetable oil**

2 medium to large **eggplants (2 to 2-1/2 pounds),** sliced horizontally into 1/2-3/4 inch thick rounds

8 to 10 large **kale leaves, washed, with the thickest portion of the center rib trimmed away but leaving enough of it to keep the leaf in one piece**

Additional **vegetable oil**

Salt and freshly ground black pepper

1. In a medium-sized bowl, combine the miso, mirin, rice wine vinegar, ginger, sugar and vegetable oil together until well blended. Thin with warm water to make a sauce that drips slowly from a spoon. You want to be able to brush it easily on the eggplant slices.

2. Place the eggplant slices on a plate in a single layer and microwave 4 to 5 minutes until just tender. Repeat until all the slices have been microwaved. Brush one side of each eggplant slice with the miso sauce and set aside.

3. Prepare a charcoal grill for one-zone direct grilling (page 5), or preheat a gas grill to medium. Allow the charcoal fire to burn down to a white ash, or moderate heat.

4. In a large bowl, toss the kale leaves with a generous amount of oil so that they are evenly coated. Season with salt and pepper. Place the whole leaves — 2 or 3 at a time — on the grill, and grill until crispy and lightly charred on both sides, about 2 to 3 minutes. They cook quickly, so keep a close eye on them. Place the kale on a serving platter as the base for the eggplant.

5. Oil the grill and place the eggplant slices miso side down. Baste the top side of the slices with the sauce and cook 12 to 15 minutes total, basting and turning carefully with a spatula throughout the grilling. Take your time; the slower they cook, the more sauce they will absorb. Continue grilling until the eggplant is a deep golden brown on each side and soft when pierced with a knife. Place them directly on the kale leaves, spoon any leftover sauce on top and serve.

Three Things to Consider When Pairing Wine with Grilled Foods

According to our wine friend Michael Franz, editor of Wine Review Online and the man responsible for the wine pairings in The Splendid Table's *How To Eat Weekends: New Recipes, Stories and Opinions from Public Radio's Award-Winning Food Show*, (Clarkson Potter, 2011) — and in full disclosure, Sally's husband — there are three primary things to consider when picking wines to serve with grilled foods:

1. Focus on Fruit: Older, earthier wines work very well with foods that are braised or roasted, but wines that are relatively young and fruity tend to pair up much better with grilled dishes. The slight impression of sweetness in a dry-but-fruity red or white wine is the perfect foil for the smoky, charred flavors from the grill.

2. Chill for the Grill: Great wines for grilled foods are not only fruity but also fresh, and freshness is dramatically affected by serving temperature. Whites work best when chilled but not so cold that their aromas and flavors lose expressiveness, so pull your bottles from the refrigerator or ice bucket 20 minutes before serving. Reds are fresher and more focused at 62 degrees than 72, so pop those into the fridge for the same 20 minutes.

3. Great Grapes: Many grape varieties can do well with grilled foods, but a dozen are true standouts. On the white side, these include Albariño, unoaked Chardonnay, Chenin Blanc, Pinot Blanc, Pinot Gris and Riesling. Among reds, Grenache, Malbec, Pinot Noir, Sangiovese, Syrah and Tempranillo are especially versatile and successful.

drinks

Summer is
the time when
one sheds one's
tensions with
one's clothes.

— *Ada Louise Huxtable*

salads, soups & sides

Composing Salads

Tossing together a salad is one of the most sensuous things you can do in the kitchen, especially if you use your hands (take a look at page 65). Anyone who thinks salads are dull is missing the point. The good ones (and that's the only kind you deserve) refresh like nothing else and keep surprising you with the unexpected, be it an ingredient, a texture, or a homey comfort.

To make the most of your salad, think outside the basic lettuce box. Consider things like chard, spinach, dandelion greens, cabbage, fresh herbs, shoots, tendrils and flowers. The more variety the better.

Textures bring life to a salad; it's about contrasts — crunch played against soft, melting against crisp. Use this as a guide when adding things like shaved raw asparagus, raw sweet corn in season, canned chickpeas and beans, seeds and nuts, and slightly under-ripe fruits, including tomatoes. Of course you can play flavors against each other as well — sweet, tart, salty, bitter. Add pieces of sweet melon, pineapple wedges, furls of salty cheese, sticks of tart green papaya, funky anchovies, bitter shreds of lemon zest, and salted nuts as accents.

Farmers' Market Salad

This is the kind of salad Lynne was raised with. Every night it was a big bowl of mixed greens — tart and mild, changing with what her mother fancied.

Dressing was never made on the side and added to the salad. Instead, dressing the salad was a ritual always done at the table. Her mother sprinkled salt and pepper on the greens, tossed them with only enough olive oil to give them a little gleam, sprinkled on a little vinegar and tossed again. Then she tasted, considered, added a little more salt, or oil, or vinegar and finally, when she deemed it done, she served it up.

We turn that salad into a main event by adding a little protein.

SERVES

4

SET-UP TIME

20 minutes
prep time

1 medium **red onion, cut into thin rounds**

4 cups **ice water**

Pale green inner leaves of large head of curly endive, or frisée or other tangy-tasting greens

Pale inner leaves of large head of escarole, romaine, cos, or an entire small head of oak leaf lettuce

1 small head **red leaf or Bibb lettuce**

2 cups **or so of raw vegetables (cucumber, green tomatoes, broccoli, sugar snap peas, corn, squash —** *you get the idea*)

1/3 cup **salted sunflower seeds or pumpkin seeds, and/or canned beans and a handful shredded cheese**

1 to 2 cups **leftover meat, soy foods, seafood or poultry (optional)**

1/2 lightly-packed cup **fresh herb leaves (parsley, basil, mint, coriander)**

Salt and freshly ground black pepper

2 to 5 tablespoons **robust and peppery extra-virgin olive oil**

2 to 5 tablespoons **good-tasting wine or cider vinegar**

1. Combine onion and ice water and refrigerate for 30 minutes.

2. Wash and thoroughly dry the greens; tear into bite-size pieces and turn into a big salad bowl.

3. Just before serving, drain the onions and pat dry. Sprinkle the greens with salt, pepper, herbs and drained onions. Add whatever additional ingredients you'd like.

4. Don't dress the salad until you're ready to serve it. At the table, toss the greens with enough oil to barely coat them, using about 2 tablespoons to start; then toss with vinegar to taste, starting with 2 tablespoons. Taste for balance as you go, making sure vinegar is assertive, but not harsh. Once the salad is where you want it, serve it up.

Dandelion and Caramelized Carrot Salad

If you can get dandelion leaves when they're tiny and in their first flush of green, they are wonderfully tart, with just a nip of bitterness. That's when they're meant for the salad bowl.

In this salad those young greens play against the sweetness of carrot strips you've caramelized in a little olive oil. Add salted pistachios and fresh goat cheese and you'll have echoes of spring in the Middle East.

If you wash and dry the greens, roll them up in toweling, and seal them in a plastic bag, they'll hold overnight in the fridge. The dressing could be done a couple of hours ahead and kept at room temperature.

COOK TO COOK: *If small dandelion greens aren't to be had, curly endive, frisée, mizuna, spring blends, or other tart greens work here.*

SALAD:

4 to 5 large handfuls (1 to 1-1/4 pounds) dandelion leaves or other tart greens, thoroughly washed and spun dry

1/2 to 2/3 cup salted, shelled pistachios

12 ounces fresh goat cheese

DRESSING:

4 to 5 tablespoons red or white wine vinegar, or sherry vinegar

1 generous tablespoon dark, grainy mustard

1/3 cup minced sweet onion (Vidalia, Walla Walla or other)

Salt and freshly ground black pepper to taste

5 to 6 tablespoons oil from the caramelized carrots, more if needed

CARROTS:

About 2/3 cup good-tasting extra-virgin olive oil

4 medium carrots, peeled and cut into thin strips about 3 inches by 1/16 inch

6 large garlic cloves, thinly sliced

1 teaspoon coarse sea salt or kosher salt, more as needed

2 to 3 generous pinches of sugar, more as needed

SERVES

4

AS A LIGHT MAIN DISH,

SERVES

6 *to* **8**

AS A STARTER; MULTIPLIES EASILY

SET-UP TIME

30 minutes prep time; 15 minutes cook time

1. Heap the greens on individual plates. Scatter with the nuts and small spoonfuls of the goat cheese.

2. To make the dressing, in a medium bowl whisk together the vinegar, mustard, onion, and salt and pepper to taste. Set aside.

3. To caramelize the carrots, place a slotted spoon and 3 or 4 layers of paper towels on a cookie sheet near the stove. In a 12-inch skillet, heat the olive oil over medium-high until hot, but not smoking. It should sizzle when a carrot piece is dropped in. Gently ease the carrots into the oil. Cook, turning with the slotted spoon, 30 to 45 seconds, or until carrots are browning. Quickly scoop them up with the slotted spoon, shaking off the oil, and spread them on the paper towels. Sprinkle them with the salt and sugar, using enough to brighten their flavors.

4. Reduce the heat to medium and stir the garlic into the oil; cook a few seconds until the garlic barely picks up color. Scoop it out and drain on the paper towels with the carrots. Remove the pan from the heat, allow the oil to cool slightly.

5. To finish the salad, barely re-warm the oil in the pan, then scatter the carrots and garlic slices over the greens. Blend 5 to 6 tablespoons of the warm — but not hot — oil from the pan into the dressing and spoon it over the salads. Serve immediately.

Yankee Tomato Salad

Straight from 19th-century American cookbooks, these big chunks of ripe beefsteak and green tomatoes (use more red ones in a pinch) get bathed in a warm, garlicky, sweet-sour dressing.

They can stand on their own, they're dynamite over grilled slabs of eggplant, pork or steak, and they make an unforgettable tomato-potato salad. Bacon fat was favored 150 years ago; olive oil works well today. Out of season, this recipe even flies with those not-so-great supermarket tomatoes on the vine.

COOK TO COOK: *This dressing can be prepared several hours ahead up to the point of adding the vinegar. Stand back when you add the vinegar to the fat, and be sure the bacon fat or oil is warm — but not hot — when the vinegar goes in.*

SERVES

4 *to* **6**

SET-UP TIME

15 minutes prep time; 15 minutes cook time

2 to 3 large, good-tasting beefsteak tomatoes (about 2-1/2 pounds), cut into 1-inch chunks

3 medium green tomatoes or more red tomatoes (1-1/2 pounds), cut into 1-inch chunks

DRESSING:

1/2 cup bacon fat or good-tasting extra-virgin olive oil

8 large cloves garlic, thinly sliced

1/4 teaspoon *each* salt and freshly ground black pepper

1 medium red onion, thinly sliced into long strips

2 packed tablespoons brown sugar

1 cup cider vinegar, boiled down by half

1/3 cup coarsely chopped fresh dill leaves

1. Gently combine the tomatoes in a large bowl. Heat the bacon fat or oil in a 10-inch skillet over medium heat. Add the garlic and a little salt and pepper. Sauté about a minute, or until garlic is softened but not browned. Stir in the onion and cook another minute just to soften slightly. Remove from the heat and stir in the sugar until melted.

2. When ready to serve, warm the onion mixture (it should not be hot). Remove from the heat, stand back and stir in the boiled-down vinegar and any liquid from the tomatoes; taste for seasoning. Pour over the tomatoes, folding in the dill. Serve immediately or at room temperature.

Golden Rice Salad

Fresh summer greens and bits of sweet red pepper dot rice the color of a sunset — this is one good-looking salad to bring to the table, or to pack away for a picnic. In fact, I first tasted it when a Spanish friend brought it to one of our "Shakespeare in the Park" picnics in New York. It's indestructible enough to go almost anywhere.

> **COOK TO COOK:** *Rice salads are so much easier than potato salads — there's no peeling steamy, unwieldy chunks. Use our shortcut for cooking rice; that is, boil it like pasta, and drain when it is done. Using expensive saffron to color the rice (its taste was lost in the cooking) is more traditional, but a little turmeric achieves nearly the same color for next to nothing. Just be judicious because turmeric is bitter.*

SERVES

4 to 6

DOUBLES EASILY

SET-UP TIME

20 minutes prep time; 15 minutes stove time

Can be made hours ahead and chilled, but serve the salad at room temperature.

1/2 red onion, cut into 1/2-inch dice

A medium bowl of ice water

1/2 teaspoon turmeric

1-1/2 cups long grain rice

DRESSING:

1 anchovy fillet, rinsed and minced (optional)

4 tablespoons Spanish sherry vinegar or white wine vinegar

5 tablespoons good-tasting extra-virgin olive oil

2 large garlic cloves, sliced paper thin

1 generous teaspoon sweet or half hot Spanish paprika (smoked or not, it's your call)

SALAD:

1 medium sweet red pepper, cut into 1/2-inch dice, or 1 large roasted red pepper

1 heaping tablespoon capers, rinsed

1/2 pound sugar snap peas, trimmed, threaded and cut into 1/2-inch pieces

Leaves stripped from 4 branches fresh thyme

Leaves from 10 sprigs parsley

1/2 cup snipped chives or scallion tops

1. Combine the onions and ice water and refrigerate 30 minutes to overnight.

2. Bring 2 quarts of generously salted water to a boil in a 4-quart pot. Drop in the turmeric and the rice. Stir, return to a boil and simmer, partially covered, about 10 minutes, or until the rice is tender, but with a little firmness left. Drain immediately in a strainer, shaking off the excess liquid. Spread the hot rice on a platter or cookie sheet to cool. It will become more tender as it cools.

3. If using the anchovy, marinate it in the vinegar in a large salad bowl while you prep the rest of the ingredients, or just put the vinegar in the bowl. Combine the olive oil, garlic and paprika in a microwave-proof bowl. Cover with a paper towel and microwave on high for 2 minutes. Scrape into the salad bowl. Gently blend in the cooled rice, drained and dried onions, red pepper and capers. At this point you could refrigerate the salad.

4. Before serving, return the salad to room temperature, then fold in the peas and herbs. Taste for seasoning, adding more vinegar or oil as needed, then serve it up.

Summer Greens & Melon Salad

You think tomatoes do a lot for a salad? Wait until you taste what cantaloupe or other melons can achieve. Why we don't use them this way all the time is a mystery.

Summer greens have an amazing range of tastes and textures — from tart to almost sweet, from crunchy to melting. You want them all in this salad. Whatever you can find in the market will make it all the better. The melon should be slightly underripe so it's almost crisp.

1 medium **red onion, cut into thin rounds**

4 cups **ice water**

About 8 cups **of salad greens, the more varied the better (like Bibb, oak leaf, mâche, mizuna, watercress, romaine, leaf lettuce, baby chard, kale, mustard, any of the escaroles, frisée, or endive).**

1/4 to 1/2 small **cantaloupe, casaba, golden honeydew, or canary melon, cut into 1 to 1-1/2-inch cubes**

1/2 cup **salted sunflower or pumpkin seeds**

1 cup **lightly packed fresh herbs (basil, mint, parsley or coriander, or a blend of any or all)**

Salt and freshly ground black pepper

2 to 3 tablespoons **good-tasting extra-virgin olive oil**

2 to 3 tablespoons **good-tasting wine or cider vinegar**

SERVES

4 *to* **6**

SET-UP TIME

15 minutes
prep time;
30 minutes
refrigeration
for onions

Dress
and serve
immediately.

1. Combine onion and ice water and refrigerate 30 minutes to rid the onion of its sharp edges.

2. Wash and thoroughly dry the greens. With your hands, tear them into bite-size pieces. Turn into a big salad bowl.

3. Just before serving, drain the onions and pat them dry. Sprinkle the greens with the melon, sunflower seeds, herbs, salt, pepper, and drained onions.

4. Don't dress the salad until you're ready to serve it. With your hands, gently toss the salad with enough oil to barely coat the greens. Use about 2 tablespoons to start. Toss with vinegar to taste, starting with 2 tablespoons. Taste for balance as you go, making sure the vinegar is assertive, but not harsh. Once the salad is where you want it, serve it up.

Cucumber Stick Salad

This has been a go-to salad for longer than we remember. Chinese in origin, it takes on nearly anything from the grill. Pair it with Smoky Salmon Steaks (page 39), Corn on the Cob with Chile-Lime Dip (page 74) and, of course, Ginger Hoisin Summer Shrimp (page 36).

COOK TO COOK: *Cutting cucumbers the night before lets them give off the liquid that usually turns cucumber salads into soup. Once the cukes have given it up and you mix the salad, you can hold the dish a couple of hours.*

8 small (5 to 6 inches long) cucumbers, peeled, halved horizontally, seeded and cut into thin sticks

1/2 teaspoon salt

2 to 3 tablespoons rice vinegar or cider vinegar, or to taste

4 teaspoons soy sauce

2 teaspoons sugar, or to taste

2 to 3 teaspoons Asian sesame oil

2 whole scallions, thinly sliced (optional)

1. The day before serving, spread the cucumbers on a towel (cotton or paper) and sprinkle them with the 1/2 teaspoon salt. Roll up the towel, seal it in a plastic bag and refrigerate overnight.

2. When ready to make the salad, turn the cucumbers into a serving bowl. Add the rice vinegar, soy sauce, sugar and sesame oil and gently toss until well combined.

3. Serve the salad lightly chilled. It could be garnished with thinly sliced whole scallions.

SERVES 8

SET-UP TIME
10 minutes prep time, with an overnight refrigerated rest for the cucumbers

Summer afternoon;
to me those have
always been the
two most beautiful
words in the
English language.

— *Henry James*

Cucumber Yogurt Salad

Think of this salad as you would a chutney. It was designed to pair with
the Weeknight Kofta with Allspice and Almonds (page 31), but would
be just as delicious with the Golden Rice Salad (page 56), Smoky Salmon
Steaks (page 39), Indian Grilled Vegetables (page 72) or just slathered
on a piece of rustic grilled bread.

1 cup **plain yogurt**

1 medium **cucumber, peeled, seeded and shredded**

1/2 **fresh green chile, minced, or to taste (optional)**

1 tight-packed tablespoon **fresh spearmint leaves, torn**

Salt and freshly ground black pepper

1. Combine all the ingredients in a medium-sized bowl and serve chilled
or at room temperature.

SERVES

4

SET-UP TIME

10 minutes

Keeps
covered
and
refrigerated
up to
3 days.

Rice Noodle and Crisp Peach Salad

Those addictive Southeast Asian noodle salads usually star Asia's crisp, sweet/tart green papaya or mango. So why not use our own summer peaches or nectarines? When they're firm and slightly underripe but still fragrant, they're ideal for salads like this.

Light, cool and refreshing, it's perfect summertime food as not a lick of heat is needed to make it. It's a good foil for Ginger Hoisin Summer Shrimp (page 36).

DRESSING:

2 large **garlic cloves, minced**

Generous **pinch hot red pepper flakes (optional)**

1/3 cup **Asian fish sauce**

1/4 to 1/3 cup **water**

1/3 cup **fresh lime juice**

1/3 to 1/2 cup **sugar, or to taste**

1/2 medium **red onion, cut into thin strips**

SALAD:

2 to 3 medium **to large slightly underripe peaches or nectarines, peeled and sliced into 3-inch by 1/2-inch sticks**

Juice of 1/2 lime

3 large **stalks bok choy cabbage, or 1/4 of a medium green cabbage, cut into 1/8-inch strips**

1 small **carrot, shaved with a vegetable peeler into strips**

8 whole **scallions, thinly sliced on the diagonal**

1 to 2 fresh **Serrano chiles, thinly sliced, or to taste**

1/2 pound **vermicelli (thin) rice noodles, soaked in very hot water to cover until soft (about 8 minutes), rinsed and drained**

1/3 cup *each* **coriander and spearmint leaves, torn**

1/2 cup **roasted cashews or peanuts**

1. Make the dressing. In a medium bowl, stir together the dressing ingredients, tasting for sweet-tart balance. Let the onions soak in the sauce.

2. Make the salad. In a large bowl, combine the peaches with the lime juice and the rest of the salad ingredients except the herbs and nuts. Chill until about 20 minutes before serving. Then toss the salad with the dressing and onions. Heap on a platter and scatter with the herbs and nuts.

SERVES

4

DOUBLES EASILY

SET-UP TIME

20 minutes prep time, plus 3 hours rest and drain for cucumbers

Make the dressing a couple of days ahead and refrigerate, but use it at room temperature. The salad can be assembled hours ahead and refrigerated, but dress it shortly before setting it out.

New Potato Salad

This could be the lightest, freshest tasting potato salad of the summer. At the farmers' market, look for newly dug potatoes, which are usually the sweetest tasting ones. You want "boiling potatoes" (as opposed to bakers) with names like Yellow Finn, German Fingerling, Rose Finn Apple, Ruby Crescent, Butterfinger, White Rose, Desiree, Red Norland or Red Bliss.

SERVES
4 to 6
CUPS:
DOUBLES
EASILY

SET-UP TIME

10 minutes prep time; 20 minutes cook time

Keeps several days in the refrigerator.

2 to 3 pounds **potatoes (see above), unpeeled**

1/2 medium **onion, cut into 1/4-inch dice**

1 clove **garlic, minced**

4 to 5 tablespoons **cider vinegar or white wine vinegar, more as needed**

1/2 teaspoon **sugar**

Salt and freshly ground black pepper

1 to 2 tablespoons **coarse, dark mustard**

2 tablespoons **extra-virgin olive oil**

1/2 cup **snipped fresh dill leaves**

1/2 cup **mayonnaise, or to taste**

1. Scrub the potatoes and simmer in water to cover until barely tender when pierced with a knife. Let simmer another 1 minute and drain. Run cold water over them for just a minute, drain and peel while warm. Cut into bite-sized pieces.

2. While the potatoes cook, stir together in a large serving bowl the onion, garlic, vinegar, sugar, salt, and pepper. Let stand until the potatoes are ready. Once they are cut and still warm, gently fold them into the vinegar mixture and let stand 30 minutes. Fold in the mustard, oil, dill, and mayonnaise. Chill.

3. Taste for tartness and seasoning just before serving. Garnish with fresh dill sprigs.

Tijuana Cole Slaw

This slaw takes off on a cabbage-onion-chile salad dressed with Mexican crema and lime that a Mexican neighbor used to make. It is delicious alongside anything grilled or frankly, tucked into a soft corn tortilla all on its own.

1/2 medium **to large red onion, thinly sliced**

1 to 2 **red or green jalapeño chiles, seeded and thinly sliced**

1 tightly packed tablespoon **brown sugar**

1 small to medium **head green cabbage, shredded (about 6 cups)**

1-1/2 cups **Ranch Dressing (page 17)**

Juice of a whole lime

Salt and freshly ground black pepper to taste

1/2 loosely packed cup **fresh coriander or mint leaves**

1. In a large bowl, toss together all the ingredients except the coriander or mint leaves. Season to taste. Refrigerate 4 hours to 2 days.

2. Just before serving, taste for seasoning and toss with the coriander or mint leaves.

salads, soups & sides

SERVES

4

DOUBLES
EASILY

SET-UP TIME

20 minutes
prep time

Cooking with Your Hands

Salads are a great introduction to a technique many chefs swear by — cooking with your clean hands. Nothing is as gentle or as sensitive to subtleties. It tunes you into your food in ways implements won't allow. For instance, only your hands can tear greens properly. Your hands tell you if there's not enough oil (the leaves feel dry when they should have the slightest suggestion of slick) or if there's too much fruit. And, most importantly, nothing is gentler in protecting fragile greens from crushing than our hands. Tongs can't come near what your hands can do.

Cumin-Scented Summer Bean Salad

This healthy salad belongs in every summer refrigerator. It's just right for a light lunch or as a side with summer's grilled fare. In hot weather, don't hesitate to open cans of organic beans rather than heating up your kitchen.

SERVES

4 *to* **6**

SET-UP TIME

15 minutes prep time plus 1 hour marinating at room temperature; 15 minutes cook time

Can be made 3 to 4 days in advance and refrigerated. Bring to room temperature before serving.

Juice of a whole large **lemon, or more to taste**

1 whole small head **very young garlic, sliced into thin strips, or 2 large mature garlic cloves, minced**

1 teaspoon **coarse salt**

1/2 teaspoon **freshly ground black pepper**

1-1/2 teaspoons **ground cumin (toasted for 2 minutes in a dry skillet)**

2 15-ounce **cans black beans or pinto beans, rinsed and drained**

1/4 cup **good-tasting extra-virgin olive oil, or to taste**

1/4 tightly packed cup **flat-leaf parsley, coarsely chopped**

1/2 tightly packed cup **fresh spearmint leaves, coarsely chopped**

1. In a large bowl, combine the lemon juice, garlic, salt, pepper and cumin. Let stand for 15 minutes. Toss in the beans with the olive oil. Let stand for an hour at room temperature, or refrigerate until about 30 minutes before serving.

2. To serve, bring the beans to room temperature. Taste for lemon, salt and pepper. Then fold in the fresh herbs. Serve cool or at room temperature.

Summer Market Gazpacho

This is a summer classic. Make large batches for lunch, supper or any time a refreshing, low-fat pick-me-up or a one-dish meal is needed. You can snack on this soup all day, especially when it's hot, humid, and the idea of actually cooking is enough to drive you to the drive-thru.

COOK TO COOK: *Do seek out the type of mild green pepper with a long, triangular shape and thin walls. Called Italian frying peppers and mild banana peppers, they have none of the domineering flavor of green bell peppers. Instead, they bring a soft, mild backdrop to the soup. If unavailable, use a quarter of a diced yellow bell pepper in the soup, saving the rest as garnish. Skip peeling and seeding tomatoes forevermore. The skin and seeds don't make them bitter, and much of their flavor is in the gel around the seeds.*

1 medium **red onion, chopped**

1 large **clove garlic, chopped**

1 medium **Italian frying pepper (or other mild, thin-walled pepper), seeded and diced**

2 tablespoons *each* **wine vinegar and Spanish sherry vinegar**

1 cup **ice cubes**

1 medium **cucumber, peeled, seeded and diced (small pickling cucumbers are even better — use 2 to 4 depending on size)**

3-1/2 pounds **ripe, medium-size, delicious tomatoes, cut into chunks**

12 fresh **Italian parsley leaves**

12 fresh **basil leaves**

Salt and freshly ground black pepper to taste

5 whole **scallions, thinly sliced**

Salt and freshly ground black pepper to taste

1. In a blender or food processor combine the onion, garlic, and half the peppers. Sprinkle with vinegar and let stand while peeling the tomatoes.

2. Add the ice to the onion mixture and process until chopped but not puréed. Add half the cucumbers, all but one tomato, the parsley and basil leaves. Process until finely chopped but still chunky. Season to taste with salt and pepper and check for balance, adding more vinegar if needed. Chill at least 1 hour. Taste again and thin with cold water if desired. Serve the gazpacho chilled but not stone cold, with bowls of the reserved cucumbers, peppers, scallions, and the remaining tomato (chopped) as garnishes.

salads, soups & sides

SERVES

6 *to* **8**

SET-UP TIME

1 hour
15 minutes
prep time,
plus
one hour
refrigeration
before
serving

Chilled Corn and Serrano Soup

This soup is a delicious lesson in frugality. The corn kernels are cut off the ears, and then simmered along with those naked cobs, onions, garlic and the snap of fresh serrano chile to make a corn-infused broth that stands at attention. Purée, chill and serve with a dollop of sour cream or yogurt and a sprinkle of chives. Or skip the dairy entirely to keep it completely vegan.

> **COOK TO COOK:** *For a smoother and more finished take on this soup, force it through a fine-mesh sieve after puréeing; discard the solids.*

SERVES
6

SET-UP TIME

5 minutes
prep time;
30 minutes
cook time,
plus
one hour
refrigeration
before
serving

Can be
made up
to 2 days
ahead and
kept
covered and
refrigerated.

4 to 5 ears of corn, shucked and trimmed

3 tablespoons unsalted butter

1 medium white or yellow onion, chopped

1 minced serrano chile, seeds removed if heat sensitive

6 cups water

1-1/2 teaspoons sea salt

Freshly ground black pepper to taste

4 cloves garlic, chopped

Sour cream or whole-milk yogurt for garnish (optional)

Minced chives for garnish (optional)

1. Cut the kernels from the cobs with a sharp knife or corn zipper and set aside. You should have 2 to 2-1/2 cups of kernels. Break the cobs into halves.

2. In a 6-quart pot, melt the butter over medium heat. Add the onion and the chile and cook until onion is softened, about 4 to 5 minutes, stirring occasionally and taking care to keep the onion from browning. Add the corn cobs, water, salt and pepper and simmer, uncovered, 15 minutes. Add the corn kernels and garlic and cook 5 minutes longer, taking care not to overcook. The corn kernels should still have crispness and the broth should smell very "corny."

3. Allow the mixture to cool. Discard the cobs and purée the soup in batches in a blender until very smooth. Use caution when blending hot liquids. Don't fill the blender more than one-third full, and be sure to hold the lid firmly in place. Taste for seasoning and adjust as needed.

4. Refrigerate at least 1 hour. Serve cool, but not stone cold. Garnish with sour cream and chives if desired.

Grilled Asparagus and Spring Onions

In this simple and unusual first course or side dish, spears of asparagus and like-shaped scallions are grilled until caramel brown and then dressed in a mustard vinaigrette.

Add quartered hard-cooked eggs to the platter along with grilled, garlicky bruschetta and you have lunch or a light supper.

1 bunch (about a pound) pencil-slim asparagus, trimmed of tough ends

2 to 3 bunches scallions, trimmed of roots and 1-1/2 inches of green tops

2 tablespoons extra-virgin olive oil

Salt and freshly ground black pepper to taste

Generous pinch sugar

DRESSING:

2 to 3 tablespoons high-quality balsamic vinegar, or 1 tablespoon each minced onion and wine vinegar

2 tablespoons coarse mustard

3 tablespoons heavy cream

2 tablespoons minced chives

1. Gently combine the asparagus and scallions with the oil, salt, pepper, and sugar.

2. Prepare a charcoal grill for one-zone direct grilling (page 5) or preheat a gas grill to high. When the grill is hot, spread out the asparagus and grill until browned and tender crisp, turning often, about 2 minutes. Remove to a serving platter, then grill the scallions the same way. Heap the scallions on the platter with the asparagus and spoon the dressing over the top.

salads, soups & sides

SERVES

4 *to* **6**

CUPS; DOUBLES EASILY

SET-UP TIME

5 minutes prep time; 5 minutes cook time

Serve hot off the grill or at room temperature.

Grilled Onion Wedges with Wine & Herbs

These generous wedges of red onion marinate in wine, olive oil and herbs, then turn crusty on the grill. Outstanding as a side dish, they could also be a meal unto themselves. We always make enough for leftovers because the onions make such a good lunch the next day with bread and cheese.

Every country cook used to have a collection of favorite onion recipes because onions grow easily in kitchen gardens and keep well through the winter in root cellars. Today they head the produce list of great bargains. Pair the onions with grilled and roasted meats like Essential Grilled Steak (page 20), and vegetables like Ginger-Grilled Miso Eggplant (page 42), or mix leftovers into our Golden Rice Salad (page 54).

SERVES

4

AS A
MAIN
DISH,

SERVES

6 *to* **8**

AS A
SIDE DISH

SET-UP TIME

10 minutes
prep time;
20 minutes
cook time

The onions
reheat well
and can be
refrigerated
up to 4 days.

1/4 cup **dry red wine**

1/4 cup **good-tasting extra-virgin olive oil**

1 tablespoon **tomato paste**

6 medium **red onions (3-1/2 to 4 pounds), cut into 4 wedges each with root end intact so the sections don't come apart**

Leaves from 3 branches **of fresh thyme**

Leaves from 2 4-inch sprigs **of fresh rosemary**

Generous 1/2 teaspoon **fennel seeds, ground**

4 large **garlic cloves, coarsely chopped**

Salt and freshly ground black pepper

1. A couple of hours before grilling, stir together the olive oil, wine and tomato paste in a large (about 8 quarts) bowl. Add the onion wedges along with the herbs and garlic. Season generously with salt and pepper and gently combine to coat the onions. Let stand 1 to 4 hours at room temperature.

2. Prepare the fire for two zones (page 5) and let coals burn until a grey ash forms. If using a gas grill, set one burner at medium-high and another at medium low.

3. Oil the grill and spread the onion wedges, with their marinade clinging to them, over the hotter side of the grill to sear for a few minutes on one side. Turn carefully with tongs or a spatula and sear the other side. Move the pieces to the cooler side of the grill. Baste with any of the marinade left in the bowl and cook for 15 to 20 minutes, turning gently for even cooking. You want them to have a little resistance when pierced with a knife. Lift them onto a platter and serve hot or at room temperature.

Indian Grilled Vegetables

Tandoori chicken inspired this grilled vegetable recipe. With the Tandoori Spice Blend (page 13) it comes together fast.

This could easily become a main dish when paired with Cucumber Yogurt Salad (page 60) and grilled Indian breads, which you can pick up in many grocery store freezer cases.

> **COOK TO COOK:** *Be sure to use organic whole-milk yogurt for the richest flavor. See pages 7 and 8 for general vegetable grilling tips. The thing to remember is that hard vegetables grill slower than soft ones. The solution is easy: cut soft vegetables thick, and cut hard ones very thin. Then everything will be on the same time line.*

SERVES

4 *to* **6**

GENEROUSLY;
DOUBLES
EASILY

SET-UP TIME

20 minutes prep time, plus one hour refrigerated marinating time; 15 to 30 minutes cook time depending upon vegetables

Serve hot or at room temperature.

MARINADE:

3 cups whole-milk organic yogurt

6 large cloves garlic, minced

2-inch piece fresh ginger, minced

3 tablespoons Tandoori Spice Blend (page 13), or more as needed

1/4 cup canola oil

VEGETABLES (USE 6 TO 8 CUPS OF ANY COMBINATION):

2 small to medium red onions, each cut into 6 wedges

3 small zucchini, cut into 1/2-inch-thick sticks

1 medium carrot, shaved or sliced to about 1/8-inch thick

1 *each* large red and yellow sweet pepper, cut into 1-inch-wide strips

1/2 small to medium head cauliflower, core intact, sliced vertically into 1/4-inch-wide slices

2 handfuls whole sugar snap peas, strings removed and tops trimmed

1 to 2 ears of corn, cut into 2-inch chunks

1. Combine yogurt, garlic, ginger, tandoori spice and oil in a bowl large enough to hold all the vegetables. Add your collection of vegetables to the mix and coat well. Refrigerate 1 hour.

2. Prepare a charcoal grill for two-zone grilling (page 5). With a gas grill, set one burner on medium-high and another on medium-low.

3. When the coals are completely covered with grey ash, lift the vegetables from the marinade (don't wipe it off) and place them over the hot side of the grill not touching each other. Take care if using peas so they don't slip through the grate. Season with salt and pepper. Grill until seared, turning with tongs. Then move the vegetables around to cook them slowly and protect them from burning. They should take 10 to 15 minutes. Test by taste or by piercing them with a knife to check for tenderness. Serve them hot or at room temperature.

Caramelized Baked Beans

This is Lynne's favorite baked bean recipe. They're unlike any baked beans we know. Sticky, sweet-tart and smoky, the beans are nearly candied as they bake with bacon, brown sugar, garlic and vinegar. A spoonful served alongside a Farmers' Market Salad (page 49) makes the perfect summer lunch.

1 pound **dried organic navy or Great Northern beans, covered with boiling water and soaked for 2 hours**

1/2 to 1 teaspoon **ground allspice**

4 large **garlic cloves, coarsely chopped**

4 medium to large **onions, chopped**

1 pound **good-quality sliced bacon, chopped**

1 1-pound **box dark brown sugar**

1/2 cup **cider vinegar, or more as needed**

1/4 to 1/3 cup **spicy, dark brown mustard**

2 teaspoons **Tabasco sauce**

Salt and freshly ground black pepper to taste

1. Drain the beans, turn them into a heavy 6-quart pot that can go into the oven, and add water to cover them by 2 inches. Stir in the allspice, 2 of the garlic cloves, and 1 of the chopped onions. Simmer, partially covered, 45 minutes to an hour, or until they are tender but not falling apart. Drain the beans, keeping their liquid. Clean the pot.

2. Set the pot over medium heat and add the bacon. Slowly cook until it has given off most of its fat, but the bacon is not crisp. Spoon off all but about 4 to 5 tablespoons of the fat. Stir in the rest of the onions and sauté them until soft. Add the remaining garlic and cook about 30 seconds. Stir in the brown sugar, vinegar, mustard, Tabasco, a good amount of black pepper, and the beans. Add about 2 cups of the reserved bean liquid, or enough to make a slightly soupy mixture. Bring to a simmer and taste for sweet-tart balance and salt.

3. Bake, covered, in a 325°F oven for 2 hours. Uncover and bake another 1 hour, or until the beans are thick and look almost glazed. As the beans bake, taste them for more vinegar and other seasonings. Serve hot. They reheat beautifully.

SERVES

6 *to* **8**

DOUBLES
EASILY

SET-UP TIME

10 minutes
prep time
plus 2 hours
soaking time;
1-1/4 hours
stovetop
cooking time;
1-1/2 hours
oven time

You could
do this
recipe a
couple of
days ahead,
refrigerate
the beans
and reheat
them in a
350°F oven
for about
40 minutes.

Corn on the Cob with Chile-Lime Dip

While we love the unabashedly decadent version of Mexican sweet corn (the one slathered with crema, cheese, chile and a jolt of lime), we also understand the need for a little restraint now and then. Consider this recipe an ascetic take, and a delicious one at that — corn grilled with just a small slather of butter until it's slightly charred then dressed with lime juice and hot chile. Utterly addicting.

COOK TO COOK: *Corn has gone through some genetic tinkering in the past, so now "super sweet" ears dominate markets. It's fine that we've got ears that don't lose their sweetness in a day, but super sweets can be so overpowering you lose that homey fresh corn taste. Look for "sweet enhanced" instead. This is from the previous generation of tinkering, and ears taste more "real" but still hold their sugars for some time in the refrigerator.*

SERVES

6

SET-UP TIME

10 minutes
prep time;
8 minutes
cook time

6 to 8 ears **fresh sweet corn, husks removed**

1-1/2 sticks **salted butter, melted**

Salt and freshly ground pepper to taste

1 cup **freshly squeezed lime juice**

1/2 cup **hot chile powder**

1. Prepare a charcoal grill for one-zone direct grilling (page 5) or preheat a gas grill to high.

2. When the coals are completely covered with grey ash, grill the corn about 4 inches from the coals, turning often with tongs and brushing them several times with the butter. After about 5 minutes, or when the corn is beginning to color, remove the cobs to a platter and give them a final light brush of butter. Sprinkle them lightly with salt and pepper.

3. Pour several tablespoons of lime juice on each person's plate, and put the chile powder in a bowl. Let the corn cool until it is easy to handle but still warm, then have everyone roll their corn in the lime juice and sprinkle it liberally with hot chile powder.

Summer Fruit Pizza
with Rosemary & Basil

sweets

Strawberries in Raspberry Sauce with Thick Crème Fraîche

SERVES
4 to 6

SET-UP TIME
10 minutes
prep time
plus 2 days
culture time
if making
homemade
crème fraîche

We have no idea if this dish comes from France, but its clever simplicity feels utterly French to us. Just take the best-tasting berries you can find and serve them with homemade crème fraîche, which in France is thick and lush naturally soured cream. In the States, we can come within striking distance of the French original by using an organic heavy cream and a sound sour cream. One caution on sour cream: Read the label. It should say "cream and culture," nothing else.

Let the strawberries "marinate" in the sauce for a couple of hours. Serve with a dollop of the crème fraîche.

2 cups **organic heavy cream**

1-1/3 cups **sour cream**

2 pints **strawberries, hulled and halved**

2 cups **fresh raspberries**

Sugar to taste

Pinch of salt

1. Make the crème fraîche two days ahead. In a clean jar, shake together the heavy cream and sour cream. Let stand at room temperature 24 hours, or until thickened. Refrigerate for another 24 hours. The cream should be thick and tangy. The longer the cream is chilled the thicker and tangier it becomes.

2. Place the strawberries in a deep bowl. Purée the raspberries with sugar to taste and a pinch of salt. Strain over the strawberries. Cover and chill for a couple of hours.

3. Serve the berries and their sauce in bowls, or serve in individual glasses topped with big dollops of the chilled cream. You could lightly sweeten the crème fraîche with a little sugar, if desired.

Granita of Fresh Pear with Candied Pineapple

You could finish a supper of beans and burgers on a high note with this dessert, or bring it in to be the finale of a fancy dinner party.

While sorbets are smooth and slick, granitas are rugged, with shaggy ice crystals and good crunch. What takes this granita out of the ordinary are the nubs of candied pineapple and spikes of black pepper. Serve it in martini glasses topped with pistachio nuts or a sprinkle of fresh rosemary.

COOK TO COOK: *If working a day ahead, let the granita freeze solid. About 4 hours before serving, partially defrost, stir and then refreeze. Stir after 40 minutes, then again after another 40 minutes. Stir a third time shortly before serving. It should be broken into shaggy crystals.*

SERVES

8

SET-UP TIME

15 minutes prep time; 2 hours freezer time

1-1/2 pounds **(4 to 5) firm-ripe Comice, Anjou, or Bartlett pears, peeled and cored**

3 to 5 tablespoons **fresh lemon juice, or to taste**

Shredded rind of half a lemon

1/2 cup **candied pineapple, cut into 1/4-inch chunks**

1/8 teaspoon **freshly ground black pepper**

1/4 cup **sugar, or to taste**

2 cups **water**

6 tablespoons **crushed pistachio nuts or small rosemary sprigs, or flowers of fresh rosemary**

1. In a food processor, blend together the pears, lemon juice, rind, pineapple, black pepper, sugar and water. Run the machine a few seconds then taste the mix for tart-sweet contrast. The flavors should be slightly exaggerated because cold will mute them. Adjust the lemon juice and sugar accordingly.

2. Continue processing until the pineapple chunks are reduced to small bits. You don't want a smooth purée.

3. Pour the pear mixture into an 8- to 10-cup freezer container and freeze. After 2 hours, stir the granita with a fork, breaking up the frozen outer rim and blending it into the slushy center. Repeat this again after about an hour, and again another hour later. You want the granita to have shaggy crystals (not at all soupy) that you can scoop up for serving.

4. To serve, scoop the granita into tall glasses. Top with spoonfuls of the crushed pistachios. If using rosemary flowers, sprinkle 1/2 teaspoon over each portion. Serve immediately.

Cool Mocha Cream

Sometimes you need a break from all that lush summer fruit with a sweet that reminds you of what good chocolate and summer cream can do for each other. The bite of strong, dark roast coffee teases out chocolate's appealingly bitter edge, so things don't go too far over the top. This desert comes together easily and holds in the fridge for several days.

2-1/2 teaspoons **unflavored gelatin**

3 tablespoons **cold water**

2-1/2 cups **heavy whipping cream (organic if possible)**

1/2 cup **sugar, or more to taste**

Pinch of salt

2 teaspoons **vanilla extract**

1/2 cup **very strong dark roast coffee**

7 ounces **bittersweet chocolate, chopped (such as Valrhona, Cluizel, Scharffen Berger, Lindt, or Guittard)**

1 cup **(8-ounce container) sour cream (not low-fat)**

Chocolate coated coffee beans or shaved chocolate for garnish

SERVES

8

HALVES OR DOUBLES EASILY

SET-UP TIME

20 minutes prep time; 5 to 8 minutes stove time; 6 to 36 hours chilling time

Make the cream up to 3 days ahead and keep it covered in the refrigerator.

1. Gather 8 coffee cups or 2/3-cup ramekins, or small wine glasses and set aside. In a small bowl, sprinkle the gelatin over the cold water. Let stand 5 minutes. In a 3-quart non-aluminum saucepan, warm the cream with the sugar, salt, and vanilla over medium-high heat. Do not let it boil.

2. Stir in the gelatin until thoroughly dissolved (you can tell by rubbing the cream between your fingers to see if there is any gritty unmelted gelatin). Take the cream off the heat and let it stand until it's warm, but not hot. Whisk in the coffee and chocolate until the cream is absolutely smooth.

3. Place the sour cream in a large bowl. Gently whisk in the cream a little at a time until smooth. Taste for sweetness, adding sugar to taste. Fill each one-serving container three-quarters full with the cream. Chill 4 to 48 hours. Serve cool, topped with chocolate-covered coffee beans or chocolate shavings.

Iced Summer Nectarines

Slices of cool, fresh nectarines take on surprisingly concentrated flavors when bathed in a nectar-like wine syrup. This is one of the more intriguing fruit desserts you'll taste, and there's nothing to it — merely nectarines, sugar, wine and an interesting technique. We've been making it every summer since I first wrote about the dish in *The Italian Country Table*.

It uses an old trick from country cooks for making decent fruit taste better and superb fruit taste luscious. Macerating sliced fruit with sugar permeates them with sweetness and concentrates their flavors while drawing out their juices into a syrup. Then, marinating the fruit in wine releases still more tastes, because certain flavors are soluble only in alcohol. Use the technique with all stone fruits, berries, pears and apples. It won't let you down.

COOK TO COOK: *If nectarines are ripe, peeling is often simply a matter of pulling back their skin with a sharp knife. If need be, dip nectarines very briefly in boiling water. The goal is solely to loosen their skins, never to cook the fruit, as its character would change drastically. Of course, you could leave their skins on as well.*

SERVES
4 *to* **6**

SET-UP TIME
10 minutes prep time, plus 7 to 9 hours marinating time

4 large **ripe, fragrant nectarines, peeled or not, pitted, and sliced into about 8 wedges each**

5 to 8 tablespoons **sugar**

About 1 cup **dry white wine (such as Pinot Grigio, Sauvignon Blanc, or Arneis)**

4 to 6 **sprigs fresh mint or lemon verbena**

1. Layer the nectarines in an attractive glass serving bowl, sprinkling each layer with a tablespoon or so of sugar. (Use less sugar rather than more.) Cover with plastic wrap and refrigerate 2 to 3 hours.

2. Taste the nectarines for sweetness, adding more sugar as needed. Pour in the wine to barely cover, turning the fruit gently with a spatula to blend. Cover again and refrigerate 4 to 6 hours.

3. Take the fruit out of the refrigerator 30 to 45 minutes before serving. Present the nectarines by spooning them and their liquid into bowls or wineglasses and finishing with sprigs of mint or lemon verbena.

Summer Fruit Pizza with Rosemary & Basil

This big, dramatic, open-face fruit tart looks like it just came off the set of an Italian country magazine shoot. Better yet, it's nearly no work. Bake the crust ahead when summer temperatures are cool. Whenever you feel like serving the dessert, slather it with the ricotta-mascarpone cream (done ahead as well) and top it with the fruit and herbs. Any single fruit or combo works, but ripe melons and stone fruits with berries are a favorite.

> **COOK TO COOK:** *A great trick to save time is to assemble the dry ingredients and the butter (cut into 1-inch chunks) for the pastry ahead of time and store it in the freezer. Write a note on the bag, "add 1 beaten egg and 2 to 3 tablespoons of water." When ready to assemble, the frozen blend goes right into the food processor. The extra chill is a little insurance against the butter melting and possibly giving you a tough crust.*

PASTRY:

1-1/2 cups unbleached, all-purpose flour (measured by dipping the measuring cup into the flour, scooping up and leveling)

Generous 1/4 teaspoon salt

1 tablespoon sugar

1 stick plus 2 tablespoons (5 ounces) cold unsalted butter, cut into chunks

1 large egg, beaten

2 to 3 tablespoons ice water, or as needed

RICOTTA-MASCARPONE TOPPING:

1-3/4 cups (15-ounce container) high-quality whole-milk ricotta

1 cup mascarpone cheese

Grated zest of 1/2 lemon

1/2 vanilla bean, split open, seeds scraped away with tip of sharp knife and reserved, or 1-1/2 teaspoons vanilla extract

1/3 cup sugar, or to taste

MAKES ONE

14 *to* **16**

-INCH PIZZA;

SERVES

8 *to* **10**

SET-UP TIME

30 to 40 minutes prep time; 15 to 20 minutes cook time

You could bake the crust up to 3 days ahead, and blend the ricotta filling up to 2 days in advance. Assemble the pizza just before serving.

Serve the pizza with a pitcher of Hibiscus Cooler (page 94).

FRUIT AND HERBS:

1/2 medium-size ripe cantaloupe, honeydew, casaba, or a mix of melons, cut into 3/4- to 1-inch pieces

2 plums or 1 nectarine, cut into wedges

1 to 1-1/2 cups berries (blueberries, raspberries, cherries, or blackberries)

10 to 12 fresh basil leaves

Leaves from a 4- to 5-inch branch of fresh rosemary

Shredded zest of 1/2 a medium orange

A few grinds of black pepper

Pinch of salt

1/3 to 1/2 cup sugar, or to taste

1. To make the pastry, combine the dry ingredients in a food processor or large bowl. Cut in the butter with rapid pulses in the processor, or rub between your fingertips, until the butter is the size of peas. Add the egg and 2 tablespoons of water. Pulse just until the dough gathers in clumps, or toss with a fork until evenly moistened. If the dough seems dry, blend in another 1 teaspoon to 1 tablespoon water. Gently gather the dough into a ball.

2. Oil a 14- to 16-inch pizza pan. Roll out the dough on a floured surface to an extremely thin 17-inch round. Place on the pan. Trim away all but 2 inches of overhanging crust. Fold it over along the edge of the pan so you have a 1-inch wide border around the edge of the pizza pan. Refrigerate 30 minutes to overnight.

3. Preheat the oven to 400°F. Line the dough with foil and weight it with raw rice or beans. Bake 10 minutes. Carefully remove the lining, prick the crust with a fork to keep it from bubbling, and continue baking another 8 minutes, or until the crust is golden brown. Cool and keep at room temperature up to 3 days.

4. To make the ricotta-mascarpone cream, put all the ingredients in a food processor and purée. Taste for sweetness and add more sugar if desired. Refrigerate until needed. Just before serving, spread the cream generously over the crust.

5. Finish the pizza by dotting the cream with the fruit. You don't want it jammed with fruit; there should be gaps where there's only the filling. Gently tear the basil leaves and lightly rub the rosemary as you scatter them over the fruit. Sprinkle the orange zest, pepper and salt over everything, along with the sugar, and serve up the pizza.

L to R: Iced Cucumber Mint Water,
Watermelon Water, Hibiscus Cooler,
Ginger-Lemon Fizz, Real Lemonade

Drinks

Simple Syrup

Open the door of our fridges in the heat of summer and you are sure to find this short-cut sweetener for any cold drink. Made from sugar and water heated together until the sugar is entirely dissolved, the syrup means no more sugar grains whirling around the bottom of your glass. Feel free to doctor this syrup with other flavors. Add a slice of ginger, a sprig of fresh lemon verbena, basil, or even the spice of peppercorns. Each addition will take the syrup to a new place.

1 cup **sugar**

1 cup **water**

1. Combine the sugar and water in a medium saucepan and place over medium-high heat, stirring occasionally until the liquid is clear and there are no remaining grains of sugar.

2. Cool and refrigerate.

variation:

Ginger-Lemon Syrup: Combine the sugar, 2 tablespoons freshly grated ginger and the water in a medium saucepan and place over medium-high heat, stirring occasionally until the liquid is clear and there are no remaining grains of sugar. Let the syrup stand 10 minutes, then strain out the ginger. Cool the syrup and stir in about 5 tablespoons freshly squeezed lemon juice, or to taste.

MAKES

1¹/₂

CUPS

SET-UP TIME

10 minutes prep time; 5 minutes cook time

Stores covered and refrigerated indefinitely.

Real Lemonade

Real lemonade is the lemonade that sends a shiver down your back when you take that first sip. It's a perfect balance of sweet, tart and cool. This recipe is based on the idea of one medium lemon per person. Adjustments are easily made depending on your love of sweetness. We like to make a simple syrup and keep it in our fridges during the summer months as it dissolves immediately in cool drinks, but any sweetener can step in — stevia, agave or even a big scoop from the sugar bowl.

COOK TO COOK: *To get the most juice from your lemons, roll them along the counter, pressing firmly with your palm to squish them a bit; or, as some Mexican pals do, zap them in a microwave for 10 seconds or so before you squeeze.*

4 medium **lemons, halved and juiced (about 1/2 to 2/3 cup juice)**

1/2 cup **Simple Syrup (page 88), or other liquid sweetener such as stevia or agave**

1 quart **cool water**

Lemon slices for garnish (optional)

1. Combine the lemon juice, simple syrup and water in a large pitcher and stir well.

2. Pour over glasses filled with ice and garnish with a slice of fresh lemon.

MAKES

1

QUART

SERVES

4 *to* **6**

SET-UP TIME

10 minutes prep time; 5 minutes cook time if making a Simple Syrup

Holds in the refrigerator 1 to 2 hours, but best when enjoyed immediately.

Real Iced Tea

According to our friend and regular contributor, tea merchant Bill Waddington of *The Teasource*, there are three ways to make real iced tea, and sun tea is not one of them. While that jar of tea steeping in the sun may look "summery," you may not feel very "summery" if bad bacteria brews. Best to try one of these three methods instead, and use that jar to store some fresh lemonade.

1. Make a regular hot tea brew but increase the amount of tea by 10 to 15 percent. For example, in a 6-cup teapot use 7 teaspoons of tea instead of 6. Strain and chill the brew in the refrigerator then serve over ice.

2. When you need iced tea for a crowd, make an iced-tea concentrate. Use 1 cup of tea for 8 cups of water. Brew for the appropriate amount of time, strain, and discard the tea leaves. To serve, dilute 1 part tea concentrate with 2 parts water.

3. For instant tea, prepare regular hot tea, increasing the amount of tea by 50 percent. For a 2-cup pot, use 2 teaspoons of tea. Pour the hot tea into a container filled to the rim with ice. Some of the ice melts and dilutes the tea while the rest cools it down.

Citrus-Mint Cooler

This cooler is an old standby at our house. With no alcohol, no sugar and lots of tart-sweet citrus, it's what to drink when the heat index is up in the stratosphere. As you sip, the mint leaves are bruised by the ice cubes just enough to let loose some of that cool snap.

3 quarts **chilled orange juice**

Freshly squeezed juice of 8 to 9 lemons

2 cups **water**

2 **limes, thinly sliced**

2 **lemons, thinly sliced**

I large **orange, thinly sliced**

One **large bunch fresh spearmint**

1. Blend the orange juice, lemon juice (start with juice of 8 lemons and sample before adding more), and water in large pitchers. Stir in citrus slices. Serve by filling glasses with ice, tucking in 2 mint sprigs and pouring in the cooler.

drinks

SERVES

14 *to* 16

SET-UP TIME

10 minutes

Ginger-Lemon Fizz and Ginger-Lemon Punch

Close to a homemade ginger ale but with more of a nip, this is a formula for an icy spiced drink made to order. Simple Syrup is steeped with fresh ginger and fresh lemon juice then mixed with sparkling water for an effervescent kick. To mellow that kick out, turn it into a punch by adding a little light rum, then relax. Drink it over ice with lemon slices and, if you like, halved stalks of lemongrass as stir sticks.

1 part **Ginger-Lemon Syrup (page 88)**

2 parts **Sparkling water**

1/2 part **light rum, or to taste (optional)**

1. In a tall ice-filled glass, combine one part Ginger-Lemon Syrup and two parts sparkling water. If making a punch, add 1/2 part light rum.

MAKES

1

DRINK

SET-UP TIME

5 minutes

Watermelon Water

We had the good fortune to spend a week in Mexico City a few years back, and while we ate killer food like madwomen, we were both entirely won over by the fruit waters, or *aguas frescas* that Mexicans routinely drink. Made daily with puréed fresh, ripe fruit, water and sugar, they are utterly enchanting and perfect for summertime sipping. You won't miss the alcohol, we promise.

> **COOK TO COOK:** *Use this recipe as a model only, as any ripe fruit will work — honeydew, muskmelon, pineapple, mango. Also, you will find that as the water sits in the refrigerator, the pulp of the fruit will float to the surface, which is totally normal. Just stir before serving.*

MAKES
1
GALLON

SET-UP TIME
10 minutes

4 to 6 cups **ripe watermelon, peeled, seeded and chopped into chunks**

1/2 cup **sugar, or to taste**

Juice of 1 **freshly squeezed lime or lemon**

1. Combine the watermelon in a blender with 3 cups of water (in batches if necessary), and blend until smooth. Add enough water to make one gallon liquid total. Add the sugar, taste and adjust as desired. Add lime juice and refrigerate. Stir before serving.

Hibiscus Cooler

Ruby red with a bright sour flavor reminiscent of rose hips (think Red Zinger tea), hibiscus flowers or *Jamaica* as it is known in Mexico, this is a refreshing and beautiful drink to brew up in the hot months. It is, in fact, filled to the brim with vitamin C and is believed to have diuretic properties to boot. Serve it on ice with a shot of Simple Syrup (page 88) to sweeten.

> **COOK TO COOK**: *According to our friend, Mexican chef Pati Jinich of PBS's* Pati's Mexican Table, *the hibiscus flowers need to be simmered, not just steeped like tea. The flowers have not been processed like tea, so they need some additional encouragement to release their full flavor.*

MAKES ABOUT
2
QUARTS;
SERVES
6 *to* **8**

PREP TIME

1 minute prep time; 15 minutes cook time

Holds in the refrigerator 1 to 2 days.

1/4 cup dried hibiscus flowers

Simple Syrup (page 88), or other liquid sweetener such as stevia or agave, as desired

1. Combine the hibiscus flowers with 1 quart of water in a medium saucepan. Bring to a simmer over medium-high heat, reduce the heat to medium, and simmer for 15 minutes.

2. Remove from the heat, cool and strain. Dilute with another 3 to 4 cups of water, then add simple syrup to taste. Serve in glasses filled with ice.

Dirty hands, iced tea, garden fragrances thick in the air and a blanket of color before me, who could ask for more?

— *Bev Adams*, Mountain Gardening

Iced Cucumber Mint Water

This water, lightly scented with fresh mint and cucumber, is sneakily refreshing. For the full treatment, serve it in a glass icy cold from the freezer. The salt brings the flavors of the cucumber up, and the longer the water steeps, the more intense the flavors become.

1/8 loosely packed cup **fresh mint leaves, washed, or to taste**

3 generous slices **of cucumber, or to taste**

A pinch **of salt**

1. Combine the mint leaves, cucumber, 1 quart cool water, and the pinch of salt in a large carafe or pitcher. Cool in the refrigerator at least 30 minutes. Serve in frosty glasses pulled from the freezer.

MAKES

1

QUART;
SERVES

4 *to* **6**

SET-UP TIME

5 minutes
prep time;
30 minutes
chilling time

Holds in the
refrigerator
up to
24 hours.

index